Peter Williamson, *French and Indian Cruelty*

Peter Williamson, *French and Indian Cruelty*

A Modern Critical Edition

Edited by
Timothy J. Shannon

EDINBURGH
University Press

Edinburgh University Press is one of the leading university presses in the UK. We publish academic books and journals in our selected subject areas across the humanities and social sciences, combining cutting-edge scholarship with high editorial and production values to produce academic works of lasting importance. For more information visit our website: edinburghuniversitypress.com

© editorial matter and organization, Timothy J. Shannon, 2023, 2024
© the text, Edinburgh University Press, 2023, 2024

Edinburgh University Press Ltd
13 Infirmary Street
Edinburgh EH1 1LT

First published in hardback by Edinburgh University Press 2023

Typeset in 10.5/13pt Sabon by
Manila Typesetting Company

A CIP record for this book is available from the British Library

ISBN 978 1 3995 0341 9 (hardback)
ISBN 978 1 3995 0342 6 (paperback)
ISBN 978 1 3995 0343 3 (webready PDF)
ISBN 978 1 3995 0344 0 (epub)

The right of Timothy J. Shannon to be identified as editor of this work has been asserted in accordance with the Copyright, Designs and Patents Act 1988 and the Copyright and Related Rights Regulations 2003 (SI No. 2498).

Contents

Editor's Introduction	vii
Suggestions for Further Reading	xxiii
Acknowledgments	xxvi
A Note on the Text	xxvii

French and Indian Cruelty Exemplified in the Life and various vicissitudes of Fortune of Peter Williamson   1

   A Discourse on Kidnapping   71

   A Short History of the Process between Peter Williamson and the Magistrates of Aberdeen   97

   Endnotes   103

Index   112

Editor's Introduction

Peter Williamson carved a singular niche for himself in the eighteenth-century British Empire. A native of Aberdeenshire, he traveled to North America as a young indentured servant and spent thirteen years there as a laborer and soldier until he was taken as a prisoner of war by a French army and its Indian allies at the outset of the Seven Years War (1756–1763). After a brief internment in Canada, he boarded a ship packed with other prisoners bound for Plymouth, England, where he arrived in November 1756. Discharged from the army four months later, he found himself nearly penniless and more than 600 miles from home. One odyssey was over, but another was just beginning.

During the course of the next year, Williamson made his way back to Scotland as a "stroller," or what we might call today a vagrant or tramp. During this trek, he struck upon a novel way of making his living: donning the dress of a North American Indian, he displayed himself in taverns and coffeehouses and told tales of his American adventures. In particular, he claimed that during the brief interlude between his indentured servitude in Pennsylvania and his military service, he had been taken captive by Indians, who had tortured him and forced him to witness similar atrocities they committed against other frontier settlers. Audiences, their curiosity piqued by news about Britain's military misfortunes in North America, paid to see Williamson's performances and to read his autobiographical narrative, *French and Indian Cruelty; Exemplified in the Life and various vicissitudes of Fortune of Peter Williamson*, which he published in York in 1757.

When Williamson finally arrived in Aberdeen in June 1758, he attracted attention by traveling around the city in a sedan chair while dressed in his Indian costume. He continued his performances and hawked copies of his narrative in the city's marketplace, but local authorities bristled at his presence. They associated strollers with thievery and other crimes and suspected that a stranger like Williamson, telling a tale of misadventures in a distant land, may very well have been trying to fleece the gullible and sympathetic for alms. But even more disturbing was a claim that Williamson made in his narrative that he had been kidnapped from Aberdeen many years earlier as part of the city's trade in indentured servants. He wrote that he had been snatched from the city's quay when only eight years old, locked up in a ship's hold among other boys taken in a similar manner, and transported to America. This trade in kidnapped youths, Williamson stated, was an open secret in Aberdeen during the 1740s, condoned by its leading citizens because they profited from it. The city's magistrates responded to these accusations by arresting Williamson for libel. In short order, they interrogated and convicted him, forced him to sign a letter of recantation, and banished him from the city. In a final insult, they seized all the copies of his narrative, cut out the offending passage, and then had the excised pages burned in front of a large crowd by the hangman. Once again, Williamson faced exile from his home town.

This time, instead of going to America, he went to court. He spent the next ten years trying to prove his identity and story, collecting depositions from witnesses about his early life in Aberdeenshire and the nature of the servant trade there. He took his case to court twice, the first time suing the magistrates who had banished him and the second time suing the merchants who had invested in the voyage that brought him to America. A tenacious litigant, he won both lawsuits and received significant financial awards from them. While this legal drama played out, Williamson continued to tour as an Indian performer in Scotland, England, and Ireland, and published new editions of *French and Indian Cruelty* that he augmented with extracts from his court cases. He became the most famous former North American Indian captive living in Great Britain, a reputation that he took great care to cultivate and promote in person and in print.

In 1760 he settled in Edinburgh and established himself as a tradesman, opening the American Coffeehouse in the Lawnmarket neighborhood of Old Town. Edinburgh was a crowded and prosperous city, the seat of the intellectual and cultural movement known as the Scottish Enlightenment. With no formal education or social connections, Williamson did not run in the same social circles as the city's most famous residents, but he sold them coffee and liquor and imbibed with them the self-improving spirit of the age. His business expanded when he opened a second coffeehouse within Parliament House, home to

Scotland's Court of Session, catering to the judges, attorneys, and clients who crowded its halls. When his legal entanglements resolved in 1768, he bought a portable printing press and learned how to use it, challenging the cartel that dominated the city's printing industry. In 1771 he married the daughter of a bookseller and went into that line of work as well. He started the city's first penny post and published its first directory, two ventures that flourished thanks to Edinburgh's growing population and economy. Although Williamson had ceased touring about in Indian dress during the 1760s, he never gave up his celebrity as a former captive. He published *The Travels of Peter Williamson, among the different Nations and Tribes of Savage Indians in America* in 1768 and exhibited Native American objects in his coffeehouses. Until his death in 1799, he was known about Edinburgh by several sobriquets that hearkened to his past adventures in the colonies, including "Indian Peter" and "King of the Indians." In person and in print, Williamson had spent his life bringing America to his fellow Britons. He was Scotland's imperial prodigal son, a sufferer of serial calamities abroad who had come home to tell the tale, a simultaneous victim of fate and a self-made man.

WILLIAMSON'S KIDNAPPING CASE

Williamson's story is remarkable, but is it true? Despite the sensationalistic stories he told about his sufferings in America, his contemporaries focused their skepticism about him on his alleged kidnapping. The magistrates and merchants of Aberdeen had compelling reasons to challenge this part of his story, as it was the central element in his lawsuits against them. Williamson's effort to prove that he had been kidnapped and sold into servitude as a child led to a prolonged legal struggle that uncovered evidence not only about his youth and emigration to America, but also about the trans-Atlantic trade in indentured servants. The archive generated by his lawsuits offers historians a rare glimpse inside a system of human trafficking that exported thousands of poor Britons to the colonies in the eighteenth century.

In January 1760, Williamson introduced to the Court of Session, Scotland's highest civil court, a lawsuit against six Aberdeen officials he held responsible for his arrest and banishment. To make his case, Williamson and his attorney Andrew Crosbie collected depositions from more than thirty witnesses who testified about his identity, family background, and the operation of the servant trade in Aberdeen during the 1740s. Not all of this testimony corroborated the story Williamson told in *French and Indian Cruelty*. A parish baptismal register indicated that he had been born in 1730, which would have made him thirteen years old at the time he left for America, rather than eight years old as he claimed in the opening pages of his narrative. A local laird attested that Williamson's family had been his tenants, and two army officers confirmed that Williamson had served under them in America, but former neighbors expressed varying degrees of confidence that the adult now claiming to be Peter Williamson was the same person they had known as a boy years earlier. Some noted that Williamson's father had fallen on hard times around 1740, after his wife had died and rising rents led to the loss of his farm. Collectively, their testimony failed to corroborate Williamson's story that his father had sent him to live in Aberdeen with an aunt so that he could attend school. Instead, a picture emerged of young Williamson living as a poor, possibly homeless child in Aberdeen with no family to support him, a likely target for merchants looking to fill up ships bound for America with indentured servants.

Other witnesses described in detail how this trade in servants worked. Merchants sent agents out into Aberdeen's streets and the countryside to find people desperate enough to consider migrating to America. In some cases, they offered immediate aid in food, clothing, and shelter to people in need of such assistance, and they promised easy labor in America and guaranteed passage home when their terms of service expired. Some witnesses claimed that these agents preyed on poor parents and their children, separating minors from their guardians and refusing to return them when so discovered. The magistrates had their own witnesses who testified that the servant trade operated in due accordance with the law, including a requirement that all indentured servants had to appear before a justice of the peace before departing for America to attest they were doing so of their own free will.

Considering the holes that all this testimony poked into the tale Williamson told in *French and Indian Cruelty*, the success of his lawsuit against the magistrates appeared doubtful until the discovery of a key piece of evidence. Walter Cochran, Aberdeen's town clerk, produced an account book kept by James Smith, who had worked as an agent for Cochran and other investors in a voyage to America by the *Planter*, a ship captained by Robert Ragg. Williamson referred to this account as the "kidnapping book" because it detailed Smith's efforts to recruit and detain servants for the *Planter* in the months before it sailed. Four entries dated in January 1743 identified Peter Williamson as one of the servants being housed and fed by Smith in a large barn in the center of Aberdeen. These entries said nothing about the kidnapping or coercion of Williamson, but they placed him among the human cargo of the *Planter*.

When the Court of Session passed judgment on the lawsuit in 1762, it decided in Williamson's favor primarily because he was only thirteen at the time the *Planter* sailed for America. According to the Transportation Act of 1718, which regulated how criminals, paupers, and other poor people might be shipped abroad as servants, the minimum age at which a person could enter into such an agreement was fifteen. Williamson may not have proved that he was snatched off the docks of Aberdeen, but the evidence he had gathered did prove that he was underage when Smith recruited him as a servant bound for America. In other words, he had been kidnapped.

Immediately after winning his case against the magistrates, Williamson sued the merchants who had invested in the *Planter*'s voyage. The first lawsuit had vindicated Williamson's story by proving (at least in the court's eyes) that he was who he said he was and that he had not libeled Aberdeen's magistrates when he stated that they were complicit in a trade in kidnapped servants. Success in the second lawsuit hinged on proving the culpability of the merchants for his kidnapping. This was harder to do for a number of reasons. Could Williamson prove that he had been held against his will by James Smith? Could he prove that he had in fact sailed on the *Planter* and was not among a number of servants who had run away before the ship departed? As this case dragged on for nearly seven years, each side sought out new witnesses and evidence, and attempted to manipulate the legal process in its favor. Williamson's reputation as a stroller and Indian impersonator did not help him as he tried to face down his social betters. The merchants' contempt for him was obvious in their description of him in court documents as someone who made his living "strolling through the country, exhibiting himself for hire in strange dresses and antic characters" and as a "mere Country Man and Clown in Aberdeen Shire."[1] Nevertheless, Williamson continued to expose unsavory details about the merchants' involvement in the servant trade and the vulnerability of children within it. His persistence paid off when he found two new witnesses, one who stated that he had seen Williamson confined aboard the *Planter* and another who had seen him sold as a servant in Philadelphia. In December 1768, the Court of Session again decided in Williamson's favor, awarding him £200 in damages, twice the amount awarded in his first lawsuit.

Although Williamson won both of his lawsuits, the testimony collected by him never proved definitively that the version of events he gave in *French and Indian Cruelty* was true. Witnesses and judges did not comment on his time as a servant, Indian captive, and soldier in America because such matters were not germane to proving that he had been kidnapped in Aberdeen. While he was alive, Williamson remained the sole authority on his life in America, leaving to historians the task of measuring his truthfulness in that regard.

WILLIAMSON IN AMERICA

Like his contemporaries, historians have not always known what to make of Williamson. Because *French and Indian Cruelty* was never published in North America, it never received the same critical scrutiny as more famous works in the American Indian captivity genre. British historians, drawn to Williamson chiefly because of his kidnapping story and colorful career in Edinburgh, have either taken him at his word regarding the Indian captivity or have retold the story with a sort of *caveat emptor* wink to their readers.[2] Archival sources on both sides of the Atlantic, however, do make it possible to reconstruct Williamson's time in America with a degree of historical certainty, revealing some remarkable truths and untruths about it.

His Indian captivity was entirely fabricated. There is not a shred of evidence in contemporary sources to support the tale he tells in *French and Indian Cruelty* about how marauding Indians attacked his home in Pennsylvania's Lehigh Valley in October 1754 and enslaved him for three months. No government records or newspaper reports corroborate his account, and the names he lists of neighbors whose tortures and deaths he witnessed appear nowhere else. The timeline he gives for his captivity (October 1754–January 1755) is one year too early to be convincing, as warfare did not erupt on the Pennsylvania frontier until after the defeat of General Edward Braddock's army at the Battle of the Monongahela in July 1755. Other narrative elements related to Williamson's captivity, such as his marriage and homestead in the Lehigh Valley, are impossible to document, and his alleged meetings with Pennsylvania's governor and Assembly after his return home are undocumented in the relevant government archives. It would appear that Williamson's Indian captivity, from beginning to end, was a figment of his imagination, manufactured with just enough detail to convince British audiences that it was truthful.

Lest we dismiss Williamson's account of his American travels entirely, it is important to acknowledge other elements of *French and Indian Cruelty*, even some seemingly far-fetched, that ring true. Williamson wrote about enduring an eleven-week Atlantic crossing, surviving a shipwreck off the coast of Cape May, New Jersey, and eventually being sold in Philadelphia to a fellow Scot named Hugh Wilson. Remarkably, all of this can be confirmed by sources found in either Scotland or America.

The *Planter* was indeed wrecked in the manner Williamson described, and its human cargo was rescued and sold a few weeks later. Hugh Wilson was a land owner who lived a few miles west of Philadelphia in Chester County, Pennsylvania, and Williamson's name appears in local tax records there in the early 1750s. But Wilson's last will and testament makes no mention of the bequest that Williamson claims his master left him, nor can any record be found of the marriage that Williamson supposedly entered into after his servitude ended. All available evidence indicates that Williamson, like many other migrants to North America in the mid-eighteenth century, lived a quiet life in Philadelphia's countryside, first as an indentured servant and then as a rural laborer, until he enlisted in the army in 1755.

According to *French and Indian Cruelty*, Williamson spent the last twenty-one months of his thirteen years in America as soldier serving in the British cause in the Seven Years War. He enlisted in the 50th Regiment, a regular army unit raised in America and commanded by William Shirley, the royal governor of Massachusetts. Pay and muster records for the regiment from this period are incomplete, making it impossible to use them to track Williamson's service, but the officers he claimed he served under and the campaigns he participated in are confirmed in other sources. The certificate he secured from two of his former officers after returning to Aberdeen confirmed the wound he wrote about receiving in *French and Indian Cruelty*. Other elements of his military service described in the narrative are fabrications. He invented a story in which he rescued a young woman from her Indian captors and another tale about serving alongside Benjamin Franklin during the famous Pennsylvanian's brief career as a militia officer. These flights of fancy aside, Williamson appears to have led a military life much like that of any other eighteenth-century redcoat, filled with mundane marching and labor, until the siege of Oswego in 1756.

The British had established Oswego on the southeastern shore of Lake Ontario in the 1720s as a post for New York's fur trade. At the outset of the Seven Years War, General Shirley sent the 50th Regiment there to improve its fortifications and prepare it as a naval base for operations against French Canada. A French and Indian force led by General Louis Joseph, marquis de Montcalm attacked Oswego in August 1756, and in an embarrassing defeat for the British, the American soldiers there capitulated with barely a fight. In a melee that followed the surrender, French-allied Indians killed some of the British civilians and soldiers who fell into their hands, a breach in the terms of capitulation that anticipated the more famous massacre at Fort William Henry a year later immortalized by James Fenimore Cooper in *Last of the Mohicans* (1826). The French marched the rest of the garrison captured at Oswego into Canada, where they were held in Quebec as prisoners of war. Williamson's description of the fall of Oswego and its aftermath jibes well with accounts in other sources. During this brief but tumultuous period, he likely encountered Native Americans for the first time and may have heard stories from other soldiers and civilians that shaped his notions about Indian captivity. Although his account of these events may strike readers as an overly dramatized ending to an already tall tale, it is arguably the most truthful part of *French and Indian Cruelty*.

FRENCH AND INDIAN CRUELTY AS LITERATURE AND HISTORY

The braiding of fact and fiction throughout Williamson's narrative renders it a problematic but fascinating historical text. Modern readers of *French and Indian Cruelty* will ask why Williamson, if he had indeed experienced many of the misfortunes detailed in its pages, would have fabricated other ones that undermined his credibility? Answering that requires placing this book within its broader cultural context as a personal narrative that blurred the line between autobiography and fiction. Early English novels such as Daniel Defoe's *Robinson Crusoe* (1719) and Jonathan Swift's *Gulliver's Travels* (1726) are famous examples of such "factual fictions," which typically featured protagonists who were shipwrecked or otherwise forced to go on travels in distant lands populated by strange peoples.[3] Other examples included captivity stories of British sailors taken by Barbary pirates in North Africa or soldiers sold into slavery after being captured by Ottoman Turks. Kidnapping stories and similar true crime tales fell into this genre as well. Edward Kimber's *The History of the Life and Adventures of Mr. Anderson. Containing His strange Varieties of Fortune in Europe and America* (1754) was a picaresque novel about a boy kidnapped from London and sold into servitude in America, where he was taken captive by Indians. The most famous kidnapping story circulating in Britain at the time of Williamson's reappearance in Aberdeen concerned James Annesley, an Anglo-Irish heir who had been spirited away from Dublin by his uncle in 1728 and sold into servitude in America. Like Williamson, Annesley returned after a thirteen-year absence and sued his uncle for the family's title and estates. *French and Indian Cruelty* also echoed the story told in *The Infortunate: or, the Voyage and Adventures of William Moraley* (1743), the autobiography of a watchmaker from Newcastle-upon-Tyne who traveled to Pennsylvania as an indentured servant and endured five years of peripatetic misadventures there before returning home.

As these other works indicate, Williamson's narrative was hardly *sui generis*. While the tale he told of serial captivities and exiles may have been unique in its circumstances, it fit readily into a literary marketplace that often featured protagonists facing trials in strange lands and that valued sensationalism over truthfulness. The public's taste for such entertainment likely explains why Williamson invented an Indian captivity to serve as the centerpiece for his story. When he returned to Britain as a repatriated prisoner of war, he was among the first eyewitnesses there to report on the military debacles British forces were experiencing in North America. Newspapers, magazines, and other public prints had whetted readers' appetites for news from America, particularly about the Native American warriors who seemed to be making such short work of British soldiers. Somewhere between Plymouth and Aberdeen, Williamson probably realized that a fabricated Indian captivity would distinguish his tale of woe from those being told by other veterans returning from America and seeking the public's sympathy.

Despite Williamson's penchant for wandering away from the truth, *French and Indian Cruelty* still has much to offer as a historical source on the experience of eighteenth-century Scots in the British Empire. It is a rare example of a "there-and-back" first person account of life in the American colonies, providing a bottom-up perspective on the experiences of migration, servitude, and military service. Even his tale of Indian captivity, as fake as it is, can be read as evidence of how the Seven Years War in North America affected the British public's perception of Native Americans and commodified their depiction in print and live performance. The frontispiece of *French and Indian Cruelty*, which depicted Williamson in his Indian dress, first appeared in the fourth edition. The version published in the fifth edition added a legend that helped readers identify the objects and scenes associated with Native Americans that Williamson described in the pages of the narrative: a tomahawk, scalping knife, and wampum belt that were incorporated into his costume, and background scenes of a war dance, bush fighting, and Indians canoeing in a river (see Figure, overleaf). As this image indicates, Williamson's depiction of Native Americans in both his narrative and live performances emphasized the savagery that Britons associated with their methods of warfare: surprise raids on civilian homesteads, the mutilation of enemy dead, and the torture of captives (glimpsed in the background scene of a war dance around a captive tied to a tree). Such depictions placed Williamson squarely within a broader British trend during the

Peter Williamson in the Dress of a Delaware Indian. Frontispiece to *French and Indian Cruelty*, fifth edition, 1762. Image reproduced with the permission of the National Library of Scotland, shelf mark ABS.1.88.208.

Seven Years War that turned visual images, print texts, and material objects associated with Native Americans into commodities by which Britons consumed their empire.

French and Indian Cruelty also provides rare firsthand testimony about the trade in indentured servants, which flourished in England in the seventeenth century and expanded into Ireland and Scotland in the eighteenth. The early editions of *French and Indian Cruelty* featured only Williamson's voice in this regard, but starting with the third edition (1758), Williamson expanded its content to include excerpts taken from depositions he had gathered about Aberdeen's servant trade. This material is an invaluable record of how merchants and their agents recruited, housed, and fed servants until they sailed for America, and of how the young, poor, and otherwise vulnerable were often swept up into this business against their wishes. By the time Williamson published the fifth edition of *French and Indian Cruelty* in 1762, he had added approximately half of its original length with this supplemental material, creating a parallel text to his captivity narrative that served as an exposé on the servant trade. It remains an unparalleled resource for hearing from people otherwise left voiceless in the archival records of eighteenth-century migration and servitude.

The publication history of *French and Indian Cruelty* tells us something about how Williamson reached his readers. The first five editions were published between 1757 and 1762 in four cities: York (first and second editions, both in 1757), Glasgow (third edition, 1758), London (fourth edition, 1759), and Edinburgh (fifth edition, 1762). Newspaper and magazine advertisements indicate that new editions appeared when Williamson visited these cities and that he sold copies at his performances. According to testimony he provided in his lawsuit against the magistrates of Aberdeen, he printed several hundred copies at a time and sold them for a shilling each, netting a tidy income. A seventh edition appeared in Dublin in 1766 when Williamson visited Ireland. There is no record or extant copy of a sixth edition, but it was likely a pirated Irish version that preceded the Dublin edition.[4] After Williamson ceased his touring, two more editions appeared during his lifetime, both published in Edinburgh (1787 and 1792). Posthumous editions continued to appear well into the nineteenth century, typically in abridged versions under variations of the title *The Life and Adventures of Peter Williamson*. These were chapbooks that excised the material on Williamson's military career and focused on his tale of kidnapping and Indian captivity. Some were pitched as children's stories, and others as abolitionist tracts that compared the youthful Williamson's fate to the spiriting away of Africans from their homes in the Atlantic slave trade. Versions of Williamson's narrative also appeared in nineteenth-century compilations of true crime stories and similar sensationalistic tales.

On the other side of the Atlantic, Williamson's story had a different career. No complete edition of *French and Indian Cruelty* was ever published in North America. As such, the book has remained outside of the captivity narrative canon in American literature, even though it anticipated the transition from the Puritan captivity tales of the colonial era with their female heroines and devotional themes to the more lurid and violent captivity tales of the Revolutionary and early national eras, featuring male heroes such as Daniel Boone. Perhaps because of those similarities, versions of Williamson's story began appearing in the 1790s in anthologies of captivity narratives compiled by American printers, even though it predated the other narratives it appeared alongside by several decades. The earliest of these anthologies misidentified Williamson as "Peter Wilkinson," and like the British chapbook editions, it dropped the material about Williamson's military career to focus on his time among the Indians.[5]

As a writer and printer, Williamson produced a number of other publications that reflected his interest in American affairs and Edinburgh's civic culture. Capitalizing on his claim to firsthand expertise in the colonies, he published two pamphlets after his return to Britain related to the Seven Years War. *Some Considerations on the Present of Affairs* (1758) endorsed the Militia Act of 1757, a controversial measure intended by Parliament to prepare Britain for an anticipated invasion from France. A few years later, after Britain's military fortunes had improved, he published *Brief Account of the War in N. America* (1760), in which he waded into the debate over whether Britain should retain Canada as a colonial possession or return it to France. A dedicated imperialist, he favored the former. We have already noted his *Travels of Peter Williamson* (1768), which was mostly plagiarized from other travelogues of North America, and his successful Edinburgh directory, which appeared in fifteen editions between 1773 and 1794. The most engaging publication to come from his own printing press was an attempt to break into Edinburgh's periodicals market. The *Scots Spy, or Critical Observer* (1776) and the *New Scots Spy, or Critical Observer* (1777) were typical magazines of their day, compendiums of prose and verse aimed at readers interested in literature and politics, but with a bit more bawdy humor and a satirical edge. They embodied the do-it-yourself spirit of Williamson's work as a printer, but neither attracted enough advertising or subscriptions to remain viable. Williamson engaged in a different kind of exhibitionism in 1789 when he published *The Trial of Divorce, at the instance of Peter Williamson, Printer in Edinburgh, against Jean Wilson*, which documented the dissolution of his second marriage. A tawdry compilation of accusations, counter-accusations, and eyewitness testimony about adultery, drunkenness, and venereal disease, it aired Williamson's marital failings as well as those of his wife, whom he accused of conspiring with his father-in-law to steal away his directory and penny post business.

The version of *French and Indian Cruelty* reproduced in this volume is the fifth edition. It was advertised in the July 3, 1762 edition of the *Edinburgh Evening Courant* as recently published by the author and available for sale at either of his two coffeehouses. By this time, the book had swollen from its original 103 pages to 147 because of material Williamson added relating to his lawsuit against the Aberdeen magistrates. In addition to the original narrative, this edition included a "Discourse on Kidnapping," in which Williamson told his version of the events that transpired after his return to Aberdeen in 1758, amply supplemented by extracts from depositions related to his lawsuit against the magistrates, and "A Short History of the Process between Peter Williamson and the Magistrates of Aberdeen," in which Williamson informed readers about the court's decision in his favor, which had occurred earlier that year. All of this extra material led Williamson to increase the price of the book from its original one shilling to one and a half shillings or two shillings bound. Subsequent editions published during Williamson's lifetime repeated the fifth edition's format and contents.

Williamson died on January 19, 1799. Not including his fictitious American wife, he outlived three spouses whom he had married during his Edinburgh years. He was buried in the city's Calton Burial Ground, in a grave that he shared with a boy named John Scott who had died fifteen years earlier (and whose marker still stands today). Obituary notices mentioned his kidnapping and time spent among Indians in America, as well as his public service as the founder of the city's penny post and publisher of its directory. Records indicate he had four children at the time of his divorce from his second wife, a least one of whom was a daughter who followed in her mother's dressmaking trade. There is no record of any survivors at the time of his death, although newspaper advertisements did appear shortly thereafter seeking his sons John and James, presumably for the purpose of settling his estate. His burial under a gravestone bearing someone else's name is a testament to his lifelong penchant for shape-shifting in this world and perhaps primed him to continue the practice in the next one.

Although Williamson's story is not widely known today, it did leave an imprint on a handful of classics in British literature. In the picaresque novel *The Expedition of Humphry Clinker* (1771), Tobias Smollett likely based the character of Lieutenant Obadiah Lismahago, a veteran of the Seven Years War in North America and survivor of an Indian captivity there, on a reading of *French and Indian Cruelty*. Likewise, Sir Walter Scott, whose attorney father played a small role in Williamson's lawsuit against the Aberdeen merchants, incorporated the story of a kidnapped child heir into the plot of *Guy Mannering, or the Astrologer* (1815), the second of his Waverley novels. Robert Louis Stevenson told the most famous tale of a young Scotsman's abduction in *Kidnapped* (1886), and although his protagonist never makes it to America, the plot recalls young Williamson's trials and tribulations.

French and Indian Cruelty is a fascinating artifact of one Scot's engagement in the eighteenth-century British Empire. A tale of kidnapping, captivity, and warfare, it reads as a pastiche of fact and fiction, at once a product of its times and a unique testimonial of one person's struggle to make sense of circumstances over which he had little control. Like many plebian authors of his time, Williamson presents himself to his readers as a sufferer of capricious fortune. But his live performances, his dogged pursuit of his oppressors, and his cultivation of celebrity tell another tale, one of relentless self-invention inspired by the same trials experienced by thousands of his countrymen who were also swept into the tides of Britain's global expansion. His was the everyman's British Empire, warts and all.

Notes

1. *Answers for Mess. Fordyce, Cochran, Mitchell, and Barron, and for Gilbert Gerard, and David Morice, defenders, to the Petition of Peter Williamson, designing himself Merchant in Edinburgh, pursuer* ([Edinburgh]: January 2. 1765), 1–2, and Act and Commission, Peter Williamson Against William Fordyce and others, August 30, 1762, National Archives of Scotland, CS29/1769/2/10/1, 29.
2. See for example Linda Colley, *Captives: Britain, Empire, and the World, 1600–1850* (New York: Random House, 2002), 188–92.
3. See Lennard Davis, *Factual Fictions: The Origins of the English Novel* (New York: Columbia University Press, 1983); J. Paul Hunter, *Before Novels: The Cultural Contexts of Eighteenth-Century Fiction* (New York: W. W. Norton, 1990); and Patricia Meyer Spacks, *Imagining a Self: Autobiography and Novel in Eighteenth-Century England* (Cambridge, MA: Harvard University Press, 1976).

4. In a note addressed "To the Reader" on the title page of the Dublin edition, Williamson explained that a fraudulent version of his narrative had recently appeared in that city. This unauthorized version was likely the missing sixth edition. A catalogue published in Dublin in 1767 included this entry among its books for sale: "*Life of Peter Williamson* (Dublin, 1766)." This is most likely the pirated edition Williamson referenced in his own Dublin edition. See Peter Williamson, *French and Indian Cruelty, exemplified in the Life and various vicissitudes of Fortune of Peter Williamson*, 7th edition (Dublin: Adams and Ryder, 1766), and Thomas Armitage, *A catalogue of books, which will begin to the sold by auction, by the Sheriff's of the city of Dublin* ([Dublin, 1767]), 11.
5. *Affecting History of the Dreadful Distresses of Frederic Manheim's Family. To which are added, the Sufferings of John Corbly's Family, An Encounter between a White Man and Two Savages, Extraordinary Bravery of a Woman, Adventures of Capt. Isaac Stewart, Deposition of Massey Herbeson, Adventures and Sufferings of Peter Wilkinson, Remarkable Adventures of Jackson Johonnot, Account of the Destruction of the Settlements at Wyoming* (Exeter, NH: H. Ranlet, 1793).

Suggestions for Further Reading

PETER WILLIAMSON

Brown, Stephen. "Indians, Politics, and Profit: The Printing Career of Peter Williamson," in John Hinks and Catherine Armstrong (eds), *Book Trade Connections from the Seventeenth to the Twentieth Centuries* (London: British Library and New Castle, DE: Oak Knoll Press, 2005), 115–34.

Bruce-Briggs, B. "Peter Williamson: Faker," *Northern Scotland*, first series 24 (May 2004): 45–52.

Nolan, J. Bennett. "Peter Williamson in America, a Colonial Odyssey," *Pennsylvania History* 31 (January 1964): 22–9.

Shannon, Timothy J. *Indian Captive, Indian King: Peter Williamson in America and Britain* (Cambridge, MA: Harvard University Press, 2018).

Shannon, Timothy J. "King of the Indians: The Hard Fate and Curious Career of Peter Williamson," *William and Mary Quarterly*, third series, 66 (January 2009): 3–44.

Szasz, Ferenc M. "Peter Williamson and the Eighteenth-Century Scottish-American Connection," *Northern Scotland*, first series, 19 (May 1999): 47–61.

THE SERVANT TRADE

Ekirch, A. Roger. *Birthright: The True Story of the Kidnapping of Jemmy Annesley* (New York: W. W. Norton, 2010).

Ekirch, A. Roger. *Bound for America: The Transportation of British Convicts to the Colonies, 1718–1775* (Oxford: Clarendon Press, 1987).

Grubb, Farley. "Fatherless and Friendless: Factors Influencing the Flow of English Emigrant Servants," *Journal of Economic History* 52 (March 1992): 85–108.

Rinn, Jacqueline A. "Factors in Scottish emigration: a study of Scottish participation in the indentured and transportation systems of the New World in the seventeenth and eighteenth centuries" (Ph.D. dissertation: University of Aberdeen, 1979).

Salinger, Sharon. *"To Serve Well and Faithfully": Labor and Indentured Servants in Pennsylvania, 1682–1800* (Cambridge: Cambridge University Press, 1987).

Shannon, Timothy J. "A 'wicked commerce': Consent, Coercion, and Kidnapping in Aberdeen's Servant Trade," *William and Mary Quarterly*, third series, 74 (July 2017): 437–66.

Wareing, John. *Indentured Migration and the Servant Trade from London to America, 1618–1718: There is a Great Want of Servants* (New York: Oxford University Press, 2017).

BRITISH SOLDIERS IN NORTH AMERICA DURING THE SEVEN YEARS WAR

Anderson, Fred. *Crucible of War: The Seven Years' War and the Fate of Empire in British North America, 1754–1766* (New York: Knopf, 2000).

Brumwell, Stephen. *Redcoats: The British Soldier and War in the Americas, 1755–1763* (Cambridge: Cambridge University Press, 2002).

Preston, David L. *Braddock's Defeat: The Battle of the Monongahela and the Road to Revolution* (New York: Oxford University Press, 2014).

Steele, Ian K. *Betrayals: Fort William Henry and the "Massacre"* (New York: Oxford University Press, 1990).

Travers, Len. *Hodges' Scout: A Lost Patrol of the French and Indian War* (Baltimore: Johns Hopkins University Press, 2015).

Way, Peter. "Soldiers of Misfortune: New England Regulars and the Fall of Oswego, 1755–1756," *Massachusetts Historical Review* 3 (2001): 49–88.

NORTH AMERICAN INDIAN CAPTIVES AND CAPTIVITY NARRATIVES

Bumsted, J. M. "'Carried to Canada!': Perceptions of the French in British Colonial Captivity Narratives, 1690–1760," *American Review of Canadian Studies* 13:1 (1983): 79–86.

Colley, Linda. *Captives: Britain, Empire, and the World, 1600–1850* (New York: Random House, 2002).

Steele, Ian K. *Setting All the Captives Free: Capture, Adjustment, and Recollection in Allegheny Country* (Montreal and Kingston: McGill-Queen's University Press, 2013).

NATIVE AMERICANS IN EIGHTEENTH-CENTURY BRITISH LITERATURE

Bickham, Troy O. *Savages within the Empire: Representations of American Indians in Eighteenth-Century Britain* (Oxford: Clarendon Press, 2005).

Calloway, Colin G. *White People, Indians, and Highlanders: Tribal People and Colonial Encounters in Scotland and America* (New York: Oxford University Press, 2008).
Fulford, Tim. *Romantic Indians: Native Americans, British Literature, and Transatlantic Culture, 1756–1830* (New York: Oxford University Press, 2006).
Fulford, Tim and Kevin Hutchings (eds). *Native Americans and Anglo-American Culture, 1750–1850: The Indian Atlantic* (Cambridge: Cambridge University Press, 2009).

COFFEEHOUSES AND NATIVE AMERICAN PERFORMANCE IN EIGHTEENTH-CENTURY BRITAIN

Bickham, Troy O. "'A Conviction of the Reality of Things': Material Culture, North American Indians and Empire in Eighteenth-Century Britain," *Eighteenth-Century Studies* 39 (2005): 29–47.
Cowan, Brian. *The Social Life of Coffee: The Emergence of the British Coffeehouse* (New Haven: Yale University Press, 2005).
Shannon, Timothy J. "'This Wretched Scene of British Curiosity and Savage Debauchery': Performing Indian Kingship in Eighteenth-Century Britain," in Joshua David Bellin and Laura L. Mielke (eds), *Native Acts: Indian Performance, 1603–1832* (Lincoln: University of Nebraska Press, 2011), 221–47.
Thrush, Coll. *Indigenous London: Native Travelers at the Heart of Empire* (New Haven: Yale University Press, 2016).
Vaughan, Alden T. *Transatlantic Encounters: American Indians in Britain, 1500–1776* (Cambridge: Cambridge University Press, 2006).

EIGHTEENTH-CENTURY TRAVEL AND SELF-FASHIONING

Adams, Percy G. *Travelers and Travel Liars, 1660–1800* (Berkeley: University of California Press, 1962).
Carretta, Vincent. *Equiano, the African: Biography of a Self-Made Man* (New York: Penguin, 2005).
Castle, Terry. *Masquerade and Civilization: The Carnivalesque in Eighteenth-Century English Culture and Fiction* (Stanford: Stanford University Press, 1986).
Davis, Lennard. *Factual Fictions: The Origins of the English Novel* (New York: Columbia University Press, 1983).
Oberg, Michael Leroy. *Professional Indian: The American Odyssey of Eleazer Williams* (Philadelphia: University of Pennsylvania Press, 2015).
Wahrman, Dror. *The Making of the Modern Self: Identity and Culture in Eighteenth-Century England* (New Haven: Yale University Press, 2004).
Young, Alfred F. *Masquerade: The Life and Times of Deborah Sampson, Continental Soldier* (New York: Knopf, 2004).

Acknowledgments

I would like to thank the librarians and archivists at the National Library of Scotland, the National Records of Scotland, the Edinburgh City Archives, and the Edinburgh Central Library for their assistance in my research on Peter Williamson. I am also grateful to Victoria Ramsay for her assistance as a research assistant and to Gettysburg College for funding her work. My thanks as well to Ersev Ersoy and Louise Hutton at Edinburgh University Press, copy-editor Fiona Screen, and the anonymous reviewers for helping to bring this book to publication.

A Note on the Text

Original spelling and punctuation have been retained, except in instances where archaic usage or typographical errors might cause confusion. Editorial clarifications are inserted in square brackets. Footnotes are as they appeared in the original text unless otherwise noted. Endnotes are by the editor.

FRENCH and INDIAN CRUELTY;

Exemplified in the

L I F E

And various vicissitudes of Fortune

OF

PETER WILLIAMSON

Who was carried off from *Aberdeen* in his infancy, and sold as a Slave in *Pensylvania*.

CONTAINING

The History of the Author's Adventures in *N. America*; his Captivity among the Indians, and manner of his escape; the customs, dress, &c. of the Savages; military operations in that quarter; with a description of the British Settlements, &c. &c.

TO WHICH IS ADDED,

An account of the Proceedings of the Magistrates of Aberdeen against him on his return to Scotland; A brief History of his Process against them before the Court of Session, and a short Dissertation on KIDNAPPING.

The Fifth Edition, with large Improvements.

EDINBURGH:

Printed for the AUTHOR, and Sold by him at his shop in the Parliament House. MDCCLXII.

THE reader is not here to expect a large and useless detail of the transactions of late years, in that part of the world, where ever since my infancy, it has been my misfortune to have lived. Was it in my power, indeed, to set off with pompous diction, and embellish with artificial descriptions, what has so ingrossed the attention of *Europe*, as well as the scenes of action for some years past, perhaps I might; but my poor pen, being wholly unfit for such a task, and never otherwise employed than just for my own affairs and amusement, while I had the pleasure of living tranquil and undisturbed, I must beg leave to desist from such an attempt; and, if such is expected from me, claim the indulgence of that pardon which is never refused to those incapacitated of performing what may be desired of them. And, as a plain, impartial, and succinct narrative of my own life and various vicissitudes of fortune, is all I shall aim at, I shall herein confine myself to plain simple truth, and, in [t]he dictates resulting from an honest heart, give the reader no other entertainment than what shall be matter of fact; and of such things as have actually happened to me, or come to my own knowledge, in the sphere of life, in which it has been my lot to be placed. Not, but I hope may be allowed, now and then, to carry on my narrative from the informations I have received of such things as relate to my design, though they have not been done or transacted in my presence.

It being usual in narratives like this, to give a short account of the author's birth, education, and juvenile exploits, the same being looked upon as a necessary, or at least satisfactory piece of information to the curious and inquisitive reader; I shall, without boasting of a family I am no way intitled to, or recounting adventures in my youth, to which I was entirely a stranger, in a short manner, gratify such curiosity; not expecting, as I said before, to be admired for that elegance of stile and profusion of words, so universally made use of in details and histories of those adventurers, who have of late years obliged the world with their anecdotes and memoirs; and which have had scarce any other existence than in the brains of a bookseller's or printer's *Garreteer* [*Gazetteer*]; who, from fewer incidents and less surprizing matter than will be found in this short narrative, have been, and are daily enabled, to spin and work out their elaborate performances to three or four volumes. That I, like them, publish this for support, is true; but as I am too sensible, the major part of mankind will give much more to a bookseller, to be in the fashion, or satisfy their curiosity, in having or reading a new puffed up history or novel, than to a real object of distress, for an accurate and faithful account of a series of misfortunes, I have thought it more adviseable to confine myself as to size and price, than by making a larger volume, miss that assistance and relief, of which I at present am in so great need.

Know, therefore, that I was born in *Hirnley*, in the parish of *Aboyne* and county of *Aberdeen, North-Britain*; if not of rich, yet of reputable parents, who supported me in the best manner they could, as long as they had the happiness of having me under their inspection; but fatally for me, and to their great grief, as it afterwards proved, I was sent to live with an aunt at *Aberdeen*. [W]hen under the years of pupillarity[1], playing on the key [quay], with others of my companions, being of a stout robust constitution, I was taken notice of by two fellows belonging to a vessel in the harbour employed (as the trade then was) by some of the *worthy* merchants of the town, in that villainous and execrable practice called *kidnapping*; that is, stealing young children from their parents and selling them as slaves in the plantations abroad. Being marked out by those monsters of impiety as their prey, I was easily cajoled on board the ship by them, where I was no sooner got, than they conducted me between the decks, to some others they had kidnapped in the same manner. At that time, I had no sense of the fate that was destined for me, and spent the time in childish amusements with my fellow sufferers in the steerage, being never suffered to go up on deck whilst the vessel lay in the harbour; which was until such a time as they had got in their loading, with a compliment of unhappy youths for carrying on their wicked commerce.[2]

In about a month's time the ship set sail for *America*. The treatment we met with, and the trifling incidents which happened during the voyage, I hope I may be excused from relating, as not being, at that time, of an age sufficient to remark any thing more than what must occur to every one on such an occasion. However, I cannot forget, that, when we arrived on the coast we were destined for, a hard gale of wind sprung up from the S.E. [southeast] and to the captain's great surprize, (he not thinking he was near land) although having been eleven weeks on the passage, about twelve o'clock at night the ship struck on a sand bank, off Cape *May*,[3] near the capes of *Delaware*, and to the great terror and affright of the ship's company, in a small time, was almost full of water. The boat was then hoisted out, into which the captain, and his fellow villains, the crew, got with some difficulty, leaving me and my deluded companions to perish; as they then naturally concluded inevitable death to be our fate. Often in my distresses and miseries since, have I wished that such had been the consequence, when in a state of innocence! But Providence thought proper to reserve me for future trials of its goodness. Thus abandoned and deserted, without the least prospect of relief, but threatened every moment with death, did these villains leave us.

The cries, the shrieks and tears of a parcel of infants, had no effect on, or caused the least remorse in the breasts of these merciless wretches. Scarce can I say, to which to give the preference; whether to such as these, who have had the opportunity of knowing the Christian religion, or to the savages herein after discribed, who profane not the gospel, or boast of humanity; and, if they act in a more brutal and butcherly manner, yet 'tis to their enemies, for the sake of plunder and the rewards offered them; for their principles are alike; the love of sordid gain being both their motives. The ship being on a sand bank, which did not give way to let her deeper, we lay in the same deplorable condition until morning: when, though we saw the land of Cape *May*, at about a mile's distance, we knew not what would be our fate.

The wind at length abated, and the captain (unwilling to lose all her cargo) about 10 o'clock, sent some of his crew in a boat to the ship's side to bring us on shore, where we lay in a sort of a camp, made of the sails of the vessel and such other things as they could get. The provisions lasted us until we were taken in by a vessel bound to *Philadelphia*; lying on this island, as well as I can recollect, near three weeks.[4] Very little of the cargo was saved undamaged, and the vessel intirely lost.

When arrived and landed at *Philadelphia*, the capital of *Pensylvania*, the captain had soon people enough who came to buy us. He making the most of his villainous loading, after his disaster, sold us at about 16 *l.* [pounds] *per* head. What became of my unhappy companions, I never knew; but it was my lot to be sold to one of my countrymen, whose name was *Hugh Wilson*, a *North-Britain*, for the term of seven years, who had in his youth undergone the same fate as myself; having been kidnapped from St. *Johnston* in *Scotland*.[5] As I shall often have occasion to mention *Philadelphia* during the course of my adventures, I shall, in this place, give a short and concise description of the finest city in *America*, and one of the best laid out in the world.

This city would have been a capital fit for an empire, had it been built and inhabited according to the proprietor's plan. Considering its late foundation, it is a large city, and most commodiously situated between *Delaware* and *Schuylkill*, two navigable rivers. The former being two miles broad, and navigable 300 miles for small vessels. It extends in length two miles from one river to the other. There are eight long streets two miles in length, cut at right angles by sixteen others, of one mile in length, all straight and spacious. The houses are stately, very numerous, (being near 3000) and still increasing, and all carried on regularly according to the first plan. It has two fronts to the water, one on the east side facing the *Schuylkill*, and that on the west facing the *Delaware*.

The *Schuylkill* being navigable 800 miles above the falls, the eastern part is most populous, where the ware houses, some three stories high, and wharfs are numerous and convenient. All the houses have large orchards and gardens belonging to them. The merchants that reside here are numerous and wealthy, many of them keeping their coaches, &c. In the centre of the city there is a space of ten acres, whereon are built the state house, market-house, and school-house. The former is built of brick, and has a prison under it. The streets have their names from the several sorts of timber common in *Pensylvania*; as *Mulberry-street, Sassafras street, Chesnut-street, Beach street*, and *Cedar street*. The oldest church is *Christ-Church*, and has a numerous congregation; but the major part of the inhabitants, being at first Quakers, still continue so, who have several *Meeting-houses*, and may not improperly be called the church, as by law established, being the originals. The key is beautiful, and 200 feet square, to which a ship of 200 tons may lay her broad side. As the advantages this city may boast of, has rendered it one of the best trading towns out of the *British* empire; so in all probability it will increase in commerce and riches, if not prevented by party, faction, and religious feuds, which of late years have made it suffer considerably. The assemblies and courts of judicature are held here as in all capitals. The *French* have no city like it in all *America*.[6]

Happy was my lot in falling into my countryman's power, as he was, contrary to many others of his calling, a humane, worthy honest man. Having no children of his own, and commiserating my unhappy condition, he took great care of me until I was fit for business; and about the 12th year of my age, set me about little trifles; in which state I continued until my 14th year, when I was more fit for harder work. During such my idle state, seeing my fellow servants often reading and writing, it incited in me an inclination to learn, which I intimated to my master, telling him, I should be very willing to serve a year longer than the contract by which I was bound obliged me, if he would indulge me in going to school; this he readily agreed to, saying, that winter would be the best time. It being then summer, I waited with impatience for the other season; but to make some progress in my design, I got a Primmer, and learned as much from my fellow-servants as I could. At school, where I went every winter for five years, I made a tolerable proficiency, and have ever since been improving myself at leisure hours. With this good master, I continued till I was seventeen years old, when he died, and, as a reward for my faithful service, left me 200 *l*. [Pennsylvania] currency, which was then about 120 *l*. sterling, his best horse, saddle, and all his wearing appearel.[7]

Being now my own master, having money in my pocket, and all other necessaries, I employed myself in jobbing about the country, working for any that would employ me, for near seven years; when thinking I had money sufficient to follow some better way of life, I resolved to settle; but thought one step necessary thereto, was to be married; for which purpose, I applied to the daughter of a substantial planter, and found my suit was not unacceptable to her, or her father, so that matters were soon concluded upon, and we married. My father-in-law, in order to establish us in the world, in an easy, if not affluent manner, made me a deed of gift, of a tract of land, that lay (unhappily for me, as it has since proved) on the frontiers of the province of *Pensylvania*, near the forks of *Delaware*, in *Berks* county, containing about 200 acres, thirty of which were well cleared, and fit for immediate use, whereon was a good house and barn.[8] The place pleasing me well, I settled on it; and though it cost me the major part of my money, in buying stock, household-furniture, and implements for outdoor work; and happy as I was in a good wife, yet did my felicity last me not long: For about the year 1754, the *Indians* in the *French* interest, who had for a long time before ravished and destroyed other parts of *America* unmolested, I may very properly say, began to be very troublesome on the frontiers of our province, where they generally appeared in small skulking parties, with yellings, shoutings, and antic postures, instead of trumpets, and drums, committing great devestations. The *Pensylvanians* little imagined at first, that the *Indians* gu[i]lty of such outrages and violences were some of those who pretended to be in the *English* interest; which alas! proved to be too true to many of us: For like the *French* in *Europe*, without regard to faith or treaties, they suddenly break out into furious rapid outrages and devastations, but soon retire precipitately, having no stores or provisions but what they meet with in their incursions; some indeed carry a bag with biscuit, or *Indian* corn therein, but not unless they have a long march to their destined place of action. And those *French*, who were sent to dispossess us in that part of the world, being indefatigable in their duty, and continually contriving, and using all manner of ways and means to win the *Indians* to their interest, many of whom had been too negligent, and sometimes, I may say, cruelly treated by those who pretend to be their protectors and friends, found it no very difficult matter to get over to their interest, many who belonged to those nations in amity with us: especially as the rewards they gave them were so great, they paying for every scalp of an *English* person 15 *l.* sterling.

Terrible and shocking to human nature were the barbarities daily committed by the savages, and are not to be parallelled in all the volumes of history! Scarce did a day pass but some unhappy family or other fell victims to *French chicanery*, and savage cruelty. Terrible indeed it proved to me, as well as to many others; I that was now happy in an easy state of life, blessed with an affectionate and tender wife, who was possessed of all amiable qualities, to enable me to go through this world with that peace and serenity of mind, which every Christian wishes to possess, became on a sudden one of the most unhappy and deplorable of mankind; scarce can I sustain the shock which for ever recoils on me, at thinking on the last time of seeing that good woman. The fatal 2d of *October* 1754, she that day went from home to visit some of her relations; as I staid up later than usual, expecting her return, none being in the house besides myself, how great was my surprize, terror and affright, when, about eleven o'clock at night, I heard the dismal war-cry or war-whoop of the savages, which they make on such occasions, and may be expressed *Woach, woach, ha, ha, hach woach*[9], and to my inexpressible grief, soon found my house was attacked by them; I flew to the chamber-window, and perceived them to be twelve in number. They making several attempts to come in, I asked them what they wanted? They gave me no answer, but continued beating, and trying to get the door open. Judge then the condition I must be in, knowing the cruelty and merciless disposition of those savages should I fall into their hands. To escape which dreadful misfortune, having my gun loaded in my hand, I threatened them with death, if they should not desist. But how vain and fruitless are the efforts of one man against the united force of so many! And of such merciless, undaunted and blood thirsty monsters as I had here to deal with. One of them that could speak a little *English*, threatened me in return, "That if I did not come out, they would burn me alive in the house;" telling me farther what I unhappily perceived, "That they were no friends to the *English*, but if I would come out and surrender myself prisoner, they would not kill me." My terror and distraction at hearing this is not to be expressed by words, nor easily emagined by any person, unless in the same condition. Little could I depend on the promises of such creatures; and yet, if I did not, inevitable death, by being burnt alive, must be my lot. Distracted as I was in such deplorable circumstances, I chose to rely on the uncertainty of their fallacious promises, rather than meet with certain death by rejecting them; and accordingly went out of my house with my gun in my hand, not knowing what I did or that I had it. Immediately on my approach they rushed on me like so many tygers, and instantly disarmed me. Having me thus in their power, the merciless villains bound me to a tree near the door: they then went into the house and plundered and destroyed every thing there was in it, carrying off what moveables they could; the rest, together with the house, which they set fire to, was consumed before my eyes. The Barbarians not satisfied with this, set fire to my barn, stable, and out-houses, wherein were about 200 bushels of wheat, six cows, four horses, and five sheep, which underwent the same fate, being all intirely consumed to ashes. During the conflagration, to describe the thoughts, the fears, and misery that I felt, is utterly impossible, as it is even now to mention what I feel at the remembrance thereof.

Having thus finished the execrable business about which they came, one of the monsters came to me with a *Tomahawk** in his hand, threatening me with the worst of deaths, if I would not willingly go with them, and be contented with their way of living. This I seemingly agreed to, promising to do every thing for them that lay in my power; trusting to Providence for the time when I might be delivered out of their hands. Upon this they untied me, and gave me a great load to carry on my back, under which I travelled all that night with them, full of the most terrible apprehensions, and oppressed with the greatest anxiety of mind, lest my unhappy wife should likewise have fallen a prey to these cruel monsters. At day-break, my infernal masters ordered me to lay down my load, when tying my hands again round a tree with a small cord, they forced the blood out of my fingers ends. They then kindled a fire near the tree whereto I was bound, which filled me with the most dreadful agonies, concluding I was going to be made a sacrifice to their barbarity.

This narrative, O reader! may seem dry and tedious to you: My miseries and misfortunes, great as they have been may be considered only as what others have daily met with for years past; yet, on reflection, you can't help indulging me in the recital of them: For to the unfortunate and distressed, recounting our miseries, is, in some sort, an alleviation of them.

Permit me therefore to proceed; not by recounting to you the deplorable condition I then was in, for that is more than can be discribed to you, by one who thought of nothing less than being immediately put to death in the most excruciating manner these devils could invent. The fire being thus made, they for some time danced round me after their manner, with various odd motions and antic gestures, whooping,

---

* A TOMAHAWK, is a kind of hatchet, made something like our Plaisterer's hammers, about two feet long, handle and all. To take up the hatchet (or TOMAHAWK) among them, is to declare war. They generally use it after firing their guns, by rushing on their enemies, and fracturing or cleaving their sculls with it, and very seldom fail of killing at the first blow.

hollowing, and crying, in a frightful manner, as it is their custom. Having satisfied themselves in this sort of their mirth, they proceeded in a more tragical manner; taking the burning coals and sticks, flaming with fire at the ends, holding them near my face, head, hands, and feet, with a deal of monstrous pleasure and satisfaction; and at the same time threatening to burn me intirely, if I made the least noise or cried out: Thus tortured as I was, almost to death I suffered their brutal pleasure without being allowed to vent my inexpressible anguish otherwise than by shedding silent tears; even which, when these inhuman tormentors observed, with a shocking pleasure and alacrity, they would take fresh coals, and apply near my eyes, telling me my face was wet, and that they would dry it for me, which indeed they cruelly did. How I underwent these tortures I have here faintly described, has been matter of wonder to me many times; but God enabled me to wait with more than common patience for a deliverance I daily prayed for.

Having at length satisfied their brutal pleasure, they sat down round the fire, and roasted their meat, of which they had robbed my dwelling. When they had prepared it, and satisfied their voracious appetites, they offered some to me; though it is easily imagined I had but little appetite to eat, after the tortures and miseries I had undergone; yet, was I forced to seem pleased with what they offered me, lest by refusing it, they had again reassumed their hellish practices. What I could not eat, I contrived to get between the bark and the tree, where I was fixed, they having unbound my hands till they imagined I had eat all they gave me; but then they again bound me as before; in which deplorable condition was I forced to continue all that day. When the sun was set, they put out the fire, and covered the ashes with leaves, as is their usual custom, that the white people might not discover any traces or signs of their having been there.

Thus had these barbarous wretches finished their first diabolical piece of work; and shocking as it may seem to the humane *English* heart, yet what I underwent was but trifling, in comparison to the torments and miseries which I was afterwards an eye witness of being inflicted on others of my unhappy fellow creatures.

Going from thence along by the river *Susquehana* for the space of six miles, loaded as I was before, we arrived at a spot near the *Apalachian* mountains, or *Blue-Hills*[10], where they hid their plunder under logs of wood. -- And, oh, shocking to relate! From thence did these hellish monsters proceed to a neighbouring house, occupied by one *Jacob Snider*, and his unhappy family, consisting of his wife, five children, and a young man his servant.[11] They soon got admittance into the unfortunate man's house, where they immediately, without the least remorse, and with more than brutal cruelty, *scalped*† the tender parents and the unhappy children: Nor could the tears, the shrieks, or cries of these unhappy victims prevent their horrid massacre; For having thus scalped them, and plundered the house of every thing that was moveable, they set fire to the same, where the poor creatures met their final doom amidst the flames, the hellish miscreants standing at the door, or as near the house as the flames would permit them, rejoicing, and echoing back in their diabolical manner, the piercing cries, heart-rending groans, and paternal and affectionate soothings, which issued from this most horrid sacrifice of an innocent family. Sacrifice! I think I may properly call it, to the aggrandizing the ambition of a king, who wrongly stiles himself *Most Christian!* For, had these savages been never tempted with the alluring bait of all powerful gold, myself as well as hundreds of others, might still have lived most happily in our stations. If Christians countenance, nay, hire those wretches, to live in a continual repetition of plunder, rapine, murder, and conflagration, in vain are missionaries sent, or sums expended for the propagation of the gospel. But these sentiments, with many others, must before the end of this narrative occur to every humane heart. Therefore to proceed; not contented with what these infernals had already done, they still continued their inordinate villainy, in making a general conflagration of the barn and stables, together with all the corn, horses, cows, and every thing on the place.

Thinking the young man belonging to this unhappy family, would be of some service to them, in carrying part of their hellish-acquired plunder, they spared his life, and loaded him and myself with what they had here got, and again marched to the *Blue-Hills* where they stowed their goods as before. My fellow-sufferer could not long bear the cruel treatment which we were both obliged to suffer, and complaining bitterly to me, of his being unable to proceed any further, I endeavoured to console him, as much as lay in my power, to bear up under his afflictions and wait with patience, 'till, by the divine assistance, we should be delivered out of

---

† SCALPING, is taking off the skin from the top of the head; which they perform with a long knife that they hang round their neck, and always carry with them. They cut the skin round as much of the head as they think proper, sometimes quite round from the neck and forehead, then take it in their fingers and pluck it off, and often leave the unhappy creature, so served, to die in a most miserable manner. Some, who are not cut too deep in the temples or scull, live in horrid torments many hours, and sometimes a day or two after. The scalps, or skins thus taken off, they preserve and carry home in triumph, where they receive, as is said before, a considerable sum for every one.

their clutches; but all in vain, for he still continued his moans and tears, which one of the savages perceiving, as we travelled on, instantly came up to us, and with his *tomahawk*, gave him a blow on the head, which felled the unhappy youth to the ground, where they immediately *scalped* and left him. The suddenness of this murder, shocked me to that degree, that I was in a manner like a statue, being quite motionless, expecting my fate would soon be the same: However, recovering my distracted thoughts, I dissembled the uneasiness and anguish which I felt as well as I could from the Barbarians; but still, such was the terror I was under, that for some time I scarce knew the days of the week, or what I did; so that at this period, life did, indeed, become a burthen to me, and I regretted my being saved from my first persecutors, the sailors.

The horrid fact being compleated, they kept on their course near the mountains, where they lay skulking four or five days, rejoicing at the plunder and store they had get. When provisions became scarce, they made their way towards *Susquehana*; where, still to add to the many barbarities they had already committed, passing near another house inhabited by an unhappy old man, whose name was *John Adams*, with his wife and four small children; and meeting with no resistance, they immediately *scalped* the unhappy wife and her four children, before the good old man's eyes. Inhumane and horrid as this was, it did not satiate them; for when they had murdered the poor woman, they acted with her in such a brutal manner, as decency, or the remembrance of the crime, will not permit me to mention: and this even before the unhappy husband, who, not being able to avoid the sight, and incapable of affording her the least relief, intreated them to put an end to his miserable being: but they were as deaf, and regardless to the tears, prayers, and intreaties of this venerable sufferer, as they had been to those of the others, and proceeded in their hellish purpose of burning and destroying his house, barn, corn, hay, cattle, and every thing the poor man a few hours before was master of. Having saved what they thought proper from the flames, they gave the old man, feeble, weak, and in the miserable condition he then was, as well as myself, burthens to carry, and loading themselves likewise with bread and meat, pursued their journey on towards the *Great Swamp*[12]; where being arrived, they lay for eight or nine days, sometimes diverting themselves, in exercising the most atrocious and barbarous cruelties on their unhappy victim, the old man: sometimes they would strip him naked, and paint him all over with various sorts of colours, which they extracted, or made from herbs and roots: at other times they would pluck the white hairs from his venerable head, and tauntingly tell him, *He was a fool for living so long, and that they should shew him kindness in putting him out of the world*; to all which the poor creature could but vent his sighs, his tears, his moans, and intreaties, that, to my affrighted imagination, were enough to penetrate a heart of adamant, and soften the most obdurate savage. In vain, alas! were all his tears, for daily did they tire themselves with the various means they tried to torment him; sometimes tying him to a tree, and whipping him; at others, scorching his furrowed cheeks with red hot coals, and burning his legs, quite to the knees: but the good old man instead of repining, or wickedly arraigning the divine justice, like many others in such cases even in the greatest agonies, incessantly offered up his prayers to the Almighty, with the most fervent thanksgivings for his former mercies, and hoping the flames, then surrounding and burning his aged limbs, would soon send him to the blisful mansions of the just, to be a partaker of the blessings there. And, during such his pious ejaculations, his infernal plagues would come round him, mimicking his heart-rending groans, and piteous wailings. One night after he had been thus tormented, whilst he and I were sitting together condoling each other at the misfortunes and miseries we daily suffered, twenty five other *Indians* arrived, bringing with them twenty scalps and three prisoners who had unhappily fallen into their hands in *Cannocojigge*, a small town near the river *Susquehana*, chiefly inhabited by the *Irish*.[13] These prisoners gave us some shocking accounts of the murders and devastations committed in their parts. The various and complicated actions of these Barbarians would intirely fill a large volume; but what I have already written, with a few other instances which I shall select from their information, will enable the reader to guess at the horrid treatment the *English*, and *Indians* in their interest, have suffered for many years past. I shall therefore only mention in a brief manner those that suffered near the same time with myself. This party, who now joined us, had it not, I found, in their power, to begin their wickedness as soon as those who visited my habitation; the first of their tragedies being on the 25th day of *October*, 1754, when *John Lewis*, with his wife, and three small children, fell sacrifices to their cruelty, and were miserably *scalped* and murdered; his house, barn, and every thing he possessed, being burnt and destroyed. On the 28th *Jacob Miller*, with his wife and six of his family, together with every thing on his plantation, underwent the same fate. The 30th, the house, mill, barn, twenty head of cattle, two teams of horses, and every thing belonging to the unhappy *George Folke*, met with the like treatment, himself, wife, and all his miserable family, consisting of nine in number, being inhumanly *scalped*, then cut into pieces, and given to the swine, which devoured them. I shall give another instance of the numberless and unheard of barbarities they related of these savages, and proceed to their own tragical end. In short, one of the substantial traders, belonging to the province, having business that called him some miles up the country, fell into the hands of these devils, who not only *scalped* him, but immediately roasted him before he was dead; then, like *Canibals* for want of other food, eat his whole body, and of his head made what they called an *Indian* pudding.

From these few instances of savage cruelty, the deplorable situation of the defenceless inhabitants, and what they hourly suffered in that part of the globe must strike the utmost horror to a humane soul, and cause in every breath the utmost detestation, not only against the authors of such tragic scenes, but against those who thro' perfidy, inattention, or pusillanimous and erroneous principles, suffered these savages at first, unrepelled, or even unmolested to commit such outrages and incredible depredations and murders. For no torments, no barbarities that can be exercised on the human sacrifices, they get into their power, are left untried or omitted.

The three prisoners that were brought with these additional forces, constantly repining at their lot, and almost dead with their excessive hard treatment, contrived at last to make their escape; but being far from their own settlements, and not knowing the country, were soon after met by some others of the tribes or nations at war with us, and brought back to their diabolical masters, who greatly rejoiced at having them again in their infernal power. The poor creatures almost famished for want of sustenance, having had none of during the time of their elopement, were no sooner in the clutches of the Barbarians, than two of them were tied to a tree, and a great fire made round them, where they remained till they were terribly scorched and burnt; when one of the villains with his scalping knife, ript open their bellies, took out their entrails, and burnt them before their eyes, whilst the others were cutting, piercing, and tearing the flesh from their breasts, hands, arms, and legs, with red hot irons, 'till they were dead. The third unhappy victim was reserved a few hours longer, to be, if possible, sacrificed in a more cruel manner; his arms were tied close to his body, and a hole being dug deep enough for him to stand upright, he was put therein, and earth ram'd and beat in all round his body up to his, neck, so that his head only appeared above the ground; they then scalp'd him, and there let him remain for three or four hours in the greatest agonies; after which they made a small fire near his head, causing him to suffer the most excruciating torments imaginable, whilst the poor creature could only cry for mercy in killing him immediately, for his brains were boiling in his head: Inexorable to all his plaints they continued the fire, whilst shocking to behold! his eyes gushed out of their sockets; and such agonizing torments did the unhappy creature suffer for near two hours, 'till he was quite dead! They then cut off his head, and buried it with the other bodies; my task being to dig the graves, which feeble and terrified as I was, the dread of suffering the same fate, enabled me to do. I shall not here take up the reader's time, in vainly attempting to describe what I felt on such an occasion, but continue my narrative, as more equal to my abilities.

A great snow now falling, the Barbarians were a little fearful, least the white people should by their traces, find out their skulking retreats, which obliged them to make the best of their way to their winter quarters, about 200 miles farther from any plantations or inhabitants; where, after a long and tedious journey, being almost starved, I arrived with this infernal crew. The place where we were to rest, in their tongue, is called *Alamingo*.¹⁴ There they found a number of *Wigwams*‡ full of their women and children. Dancing, singing, and shooting were their general amusements; and in all their festivals and dances, they relate what successes they have had, and what damages they have sustained in their expeditions; in which I became part of their theme. The severity of the cold increasing, they stript me of my cloaths for their own use, and gave me such as they usually wore themselves, being a piece of blanket, a pair of *Mogganes*, or shoes, with a yard of coarse cloth, to put round me instead of breeches. To describe their dress and manner of living may not be altogether unacceptable to some of my readers, but as the size of this book will not permit me to be so particular as I might otherwise be, I shall just observe;

That they in general wear a white blanket, which in war time they paint with various figures; but particularly the leaves of trees, in order to deceive their enemies when in the woods. Their Mogganes are made of deer-skins, and the best sort have them bound round the edges with little beads and ribbands. On their legs they wear pieces of blue cloth for stockings, something like our soldiers spatterdashes; they reach higher than their knees, but not lower than their ancles; they esteem them easy to run in. Breeches they never wear, but instead thereof two pieces of linen, one before and another behind. The better sort have shirts of the finest linen they can get, and to these some wear ruffles; but these they never put on, till they have painted them of various colours, which they get from the Pecone root, bark of trees, and never pull them off to wash,

---

‡ WIGWAMS, are the names they give their houses, which are no more than little huts, made with three or four forked stakes drove into the ground, and cover'd with deer or other skins; or for want of them with large leaves and earth.

but wear them till they fall in pieces. They are very proud, and take great delight in wearing trinkets; such as silver plates round their wrists and necks, with several strings of *Wampum* (which is made of cotton, interwove with pebbles, cockleshells, &c) down to their breasts; and from their ears and noses they have rings and beads, which hang dangling an inch or two. The men have no beards, to prevent which they use certain instruments and tricks as soon as it begins to grow. The hair of their heads is managed differently, some pluck out and destroy all, except a lock hanging from the crown of the head, which they interweave with *Wampum* and feathers of various colours. The women wear it very long, twisted down their backs, with beads, feathers, and *Wampum*; and on their heads most of them wear little coronets of brass or copper: round their middle they wear a blanket instead of a petticoat. The females are very chaste, and constant to their husbands; and if any young maiden should happen to have a child before marriage, she is never esteemed afterwards. As for their food they get it chiefly by hunting and shooting, and boil, broil, or roast all the meat they eat. Their standing dish consists of *Indian* corn soaked then bruis'd and boiled over a gentle fire, for ten or twelve hours. Their bread is likewise made of this, wild oats, or sunflower seeds. Set meals they never regard, but eat when they are hungry. Their gun, *Tomahawk*, scalping knife, powder and shot, are all they have to carry with them in time of war; bows and arrows being seldom used by them. They generally in war decline open engagements; bush-fighting or skulking is their discipline; and they are brave when engaged, having great fortitude in enduring tortures and death. No people have a greater love of liberty, or affection to their relations; but they are the most implacably vindictive people upon the earth, for they revenge the death of any relation, or any great affront, whenever occasion presents, let the distance of time or place be never so remote. To all which I may add what the reader has already observed, that they are inhumanly cruel. But, some *other* nations might be more happy, if, in some instances, they copied them, and made *wise conduct, courage, and personal strength*, the *chief* recommendations for war-captains, or *Werowances*, as they call them. In times of peace they visit the plantations inhabited by the whites, to whom they sell baskets, ladles, spoons, and other such trifles, which they are very expert in making. When night comes, if admitted into any house, they beg leave to lie down by the fire-side, chusing that place rather than any other, which is seldom refused them, if sober, for then they are honest; but if drunk, are very dangerous and troublesome, if people enough are not in the house to quell them. Nor would they at any time be guilty of such barbarous depredations as they are, did not those calling themselves Christians, intice them thereto with strong liquors, which they are vastly fond of; as well as by the pecuniary rewards which they give for the scalps. If ambition cannot be gratified, or superiority obtained, otherwise than by the deaths of thousands; would it not, in those who seek such airy phantoms, and are so inordinately fond of their fellow creatures lives, favour a little more of humanity to have them killed instantly, and, if they must have proofs of murder, scalped afterwards? than by allowing and encouraging such merciless treatment, render themselves as obnoxious, cruel, and barbarous, to a humane mind, as the very savages themselves. However, they sometimes suffer by their plots and chicanery laid for the destruction of others; it often happening that the traders or emissaries sent to allure them to the execution of their schemes, rightly fall victims themselves; for, as they always carry with them horse-loads of rum, which the *Indians* are fond of, they soon get drunk, quarrelsome, and wicked, and, in their fury, often kill and destroy their tempters: A just reward for their wicked designs! nay, it has such an effect on them, that when so intoxicated, they even burn and consume all their own effects, beating, wounding, and sometimes killing their wives and children: But, in disputes among themselves when sober, they are very tenacious of decorum, never allowing more than one to speak at a time. Prophane swearing they know not in their own language how to express, but are very fond of the *French* and *English* oaths.

The old people, who are by age and infirmities rendered incapable of being serviceable to the community, they put out of the world in a barbarous and extraordinary manner; an instance of which I had whilst among them, an opportunity of seeing, practiced on an old *Indian*. He being, through age, feeble and weak, and his eyes failing him so that he was unable to get his living either by hunting or shooting; he was summoned to appear before several of the leading ones, who were to be his judges. Before whom being come, and having nothing to say for himself, (as how indeed could he prove himself to be young) they very formally, and with a seeming degree of compassion, passed sentence on him to be put to death. This was soon after executed on him in the following manner: He was tied naked to a tree, and a boy who was to be his executioner, stood ready with a *Tomahawk* in his hands; to beat his brains out: but when the young monster came to inflict the sentence he was so short of stature that he could not lift the *Tomahawk* high enough; upon which he was held up by some others, a great concourse being present; and then, though the youth devil laid on with all his strength, he was not for some time able to fracture the old man's scull, so that it was near an hour before he was dead. Thus are they from their youth inured to barbarity!

When they found no remains of life in him, they put him into a hole dug in the ground for that purpose, in which he stood upright. Into his left-hand they put an old gun, and hung a small powder horn and short-bag about his shoulders, and a string of wampum round his neck; and into his right hand a little silk purse with a bit of money in it; then filled the hole round, and covered him over with earth. This I found to be the usual manner of treating the old of both sexes; only that the women are killed by young girls, and put into the ground with nothing but a ladle in one hand, and a wooden dish in the other.[15]

They are very strict in punishing offenders, especially such as commit crimes against any of the royal families. They never hang any: but those sentenced to death are generally bound to a stake, and a great fire made round them: but not so near as to burn them immediately, for they sometimes remain roasting in the middle of the flames for two or three days before they are dead.

After this long digression, it is time to return to the detail of my own affairs. At *Alamingo* was I kept near two months, until the snow was off the ground. A long time to be amongst such creatures, and naked as I almost was. Whatever thoughts I might have of making my escape, to carry them into execution was impracticable, being so far from any plantations or white people, and the severe weather rendering my limbs in a manner quite stiff and motionless; however I contrived to defend myself against the inclemency of the weather as well as I could, by making myself a little *Wigwam*, with the bark of the trees, covering the same with earth, which made it resemble a cave; and, to prevent the ill effects of the cold which penetrated into it, I was forced to keep a good fire always near the door.

Thus did I for near two months endure such hardships of cold and hunger as had hitherto been unknown to me. My liberty of going about was, indeed, more than I could have expected, but they well knew the impracticability of my eloping from them. Seeing me outwardly easy and submissive, they would sometimes give me a little meat, but my chief food was *Indian* corn, dressed as I have above described. Notwithstanding such their civility, the time passed so tedious on that I almost began to dispair of ever regaining my liberty, or seeing my few relations again; which, with the anxiety and pain I suffered on account of my dear wife, often gave me inexpressible concern.

At length the time arrived when they were preparing themselves for another expedition against the planters and white people; but before they set out, they were joined by many other *Indians* from fort *Du Quesne*[16], well stored with powder and ball they had received from the *French*.

As soon as the snow was quite gone, and no traces of their vile footsteps could be perceived, they set forth on their journey towards the back parts of the province of *Pensylvania*, and leaving their wives and children behind in their *Wigwams*. They were now a terrible and formidable body, amounting to near 150. My duty was to carry what they thought proper to load me with, but they never intrusted me with a gun. We marched on several days without any thing particular occurring, almost famished for want of provisions; for my part I had nothing but a few stalks of *Indian* corn, which I was glad to eat dry: Nor did the *Indians* themselves fare much better, for as we drew near the plantations they were afraid to kill any game, least the noise of their guns should alarm the inhabitants.

When we again arrived at the *Blue Hills*[17], about 30 miles from *Cannocojigge* the *Irish* settlement before-mentioned, we encamped for three days, though God knows we had neither tents, nor any thing else to defend us from the inclemency of the air, having nothing to lie on by night but the grass. Their usual method of lodging, pitching, or encamping, by night, being in parcels of ten or twelve men to a fire, where they lie upon the grass or bushes, wrapt up in a blanket, with their feet to the fire.

During our stay here a sort of council of war was held, when it was agreed to divide themselves into companies of about twenty men each; after which every captain marched with his party where he thought proper. I still belonged to my old masters, but was left behind on the mountains with ten *Indians*, to stay until the rest should return; not thinking it proper to carry me nearer to *Cannocojigge*, or the other plantations.

Here being left I began to meditate on my escape, and though I knew the country round extremely well, having been often thereabouts, with my companions hunting deer, and other beasts; yet was I very cautious of giving the least suspicions of such my intentions. However the third day after the grand body left us, my companions or keepers thought proper to visit the mountains in search of game for their subsistance, leaving me bound in such a manner that I could not escape: At night when they returned, having unbound me, we all sat down together to supper on two Pole Cats, being what they had killed, and soon after (being greatly fatigued with their day's excursion) they composed themselves to rest as usual. Observing them to be in that somniferous state, I tried various ways to see whether it was a scheme to prove my intentions or not, but after making a noise and walking about, sometimes touching them with my feet, I found there was no fallacy. My heart then exulted with joy at seeing a time come that I might in all probability be delivered from my captivity; but this joy was soon damped by the dread of being discovered by them, or taken by any straggling parties. To prevent which I resolved it possible to get one of their guns, and, if discovered, to die in my defence rather than be taken; for that purpose I made various efforts to get one from under their heads (where they always secured them,) but in vain. Frustrated in this my first essay towards regaining my liberty, I dreaded the thoughts of carrying my design into execution: yet, after a little consideration, and trusting myself to the divine protection, I set forwards naked and defenceless as I was. A rash and dangerous enterprize! Such was my terror, however, that in going from them I halted and paused every four or five yards, looking fearfully towards the spot where I had left them, lest they should awake and miss me; but when I was about two hundred yards from them, I mended my pace and made as much haste as I could to the foot of the mountains; when on a sudden I was struck with the greatest terror and amaze at hearing the wood-cry, as it is called, and may be expressed *Jo-hau! Jo-hau!* which the savages I had left were making, accompanied with the most hideous cries and howlings they could utter. The bellowing of lyons, the shrieks of hyenas, or the roaring of tygers, would have been music to my ears, in comparison to the sounds that then saluted them. They having now missed their charge, I concluded that they would soon separate themselves and hie in quest of me. The more my terror increased the faster did I push on, and scarce knowing where I trod, drove through the woods with the utmost precipitation, sometimes falling and bruising myself, cutting my feet and legs against the stones, in a miserable manner; but though faint and maimed as I was I continued my flight until the break of day, when without having any thing to sustain nature but a little corn left, I crept into a hollow tree, in which I lay very snug, and returned my prayers and thanks to the Divine Being, that had thus far favoured my escape. But my repose was in a few hours destroyed at hearing the voices of the savages near the place where I was hid, threatening and talking how they would use me, if they got me again; that I was before too sensible of, to have the least rest either in body or mind since I had left them. However they at last left the spot where I heard them, and I remained in my circular asylum all that day without further molestation.

At night I ventured forwards again, frightened and trembling at every bush I past, thinking each twig that touched me to be a savage. The third day I concealed myself in the like manner, and at night I travelled on in the same deplorable condition keeping off the main road used by the *Indians*, as much as possible, which made my journey many miles longer, and more painful and irksome than I can express. But how shall I describe the fear, terror, and shock, that I felt on the fourth night, when, by the rustling I made among the leaves, a party of *Indians*, that lay round a small fire which I did not perceive, started from the ground, and seizing their arms run from the fire amongst the woods. Whether to move forward or rest where I was I knew not, so distracted was my imagination. In this melancholy state revolving in my thoughts the now inevitable fate I thought waited on me, to my great consternation and joy I was relieved by a parcel of swine that made towards the place I guessed the savages to be; who, on seeing the hogs, conjectured that their alarm had been occasioned by them, and very merrily returned to the fire, and lay down to sleep as before.[18] As soon as I perceived my enemies so disposed of, with more cautious step and silent tread I pursued my course, sweating (though winter and severely cold) with the fear I had been just relieved from. Bruised, cut, mangled, and terrified as I was, I still, through the divine assistance, was enabled to pursue my journey until break of day, when thinking myself far off from any of these miscreants I so much dreaded, I lay down under a great log, and slept undisturbed until about noon, when getting up I reached the summit of a great hill, with some difficulty, and looking out if I could spy any habitations of white people, to my unutterable joy I saw some, which I guessed to be about ten miles distance.

This pleasure was in some measure abated, by not being able to get among them that night. Therefore, when evening approached, I again recommended myself to the Almighty, and composed my wearied mangled limbs to rest. In the morning as soon as I awoke, I continued my journy towards the nearest cleared lands I had seen the day before, and about four o'clock in the afternoon arrived at the house of *John Bell*, an old acquaintance, where, knocking at the door, his wife, who opened it, seeing me in such a frightful condition, flew from me like lightening screaming into the house. This alarmed the whole family, who immediately fled to their arms, and I was soon accosted by the master with his gun in his hand. But on my assuring him of my innocence as to any wicked intentions, and making myself known (for he before took me to be an *Indian*) he immediately caressed me, as did all his family, with a deal of friendship at finding me alive; they having all been informed of my being murdered by the savages some months before. No longer now able to support my fatigued and worn out spirits I fainted and fell to the ground. From which state having recovered me, and perceiving the weak and famished condition I then was in, they soon gave me some refreshment, but let me partake of it very sparingly, fearing the ill effects too much at once would have on me. They for two or three nights very affectionately supplied me with all necessaries, and carefully attended me until my spirits and limbs were pretty well recruited, and I thought myself able to ride, when I borrowed of these good people (whose kindness merits my most grateful returns) a horse and some clothes, and set forward for my father-in-law's[19] house in *Chester* county, about 140 miles from thence, where I arrived on the 4th day of *January* 1755, but scarce one of the family could credit their eyes, believing with the people I had lately left, that I had fallen prey to the *Indians*.

Great was the joy and satisfaction wherewith I was received and embraced by the whole family; but, oh, what was my anguish and trouble, when on enquiring for my dear wife I found she had been dead two months. This fatal news, as every humane reader must imagine, greatly lessened the joy and rapture I otherwise should have felt at my deliverance from the dreadful state and captivity I had been in.

The news of my happy arrival at my father-in-law's house, after so long and strange an absence, was soon spread round the neighbouring plantations by the country people who continually visited me, being very desirous of hearing and eagerly enquiring an account of my treatment and manner of living among the *Indians*. In all which I satisfied them. Soon after this my arrival I was sent for by his excellency Mr. *Morris*[20], the governor, a worthy gentleman, who examined me very particularly as to all incidents relating to my captivity, and especially in regard to the *Indians*, who had first taken me away, whether they were *French* or *English* parties. I assured his excellency they were of those who professed themselves to be friends of the former; and informed him of the many barbarous and inhuman actions I had been witness to among them, on the frontiers of the province; and also that they were daily increasing by others of our pretended friends joining them; that they were all well supplied by the *French* with arms and ammunition, and greatly encouraged by them in their continual excursions and barbarities, not only in having extraordinary premiums for such scalps as they should take and carry home with them at their return, but great presents of all kinds, besides rum, powder, ball, &c. before they sallied forth. Having satisfied his excellency in such particulars as he requested, the same being put into writing, I swore to the contents thereof, as may be seen by those who doubt of my veracity in the public papers of that time, as well in *England* as in *Philadelphia*.[21] Having done with me, Mr. *Morris* gave me three pounds, and sent the affidavit to the assembly who were then sitting in the state-house at *Philadelphia*, concluding on proper measures to check the depredations of the savages, and put a stop to the barbarous hostilities of the destressed inhabitants, who daily suffered death in a most deplorable condition; besides being obliged to abscond their plantations, and the country being left destitute for several hundred miles on the frontiers, and the poor sufferers could have no relief, by reason of the disputes between the governor and the assembly. The former was led by the instructions of the proprietor[22], which was intirely against the interest of the province, so that it caused great confusion among the people to see the country so destroyed, and no preparations making for its defence.

However on receiving this intelligence from his excellency, they immediately sent for me. When I arrived I was conducted into the lower-house, where the assembly then sat, and was there interrogated by the speaker, very particularly as to all I had before given the governor an account of. This my first examination lasted three hours. The next day I underwent a second for about an hour and a half, when I was courteously dismissed, with a promise that all proper methods should be taken, not only to accommodate and reimburse all those who had suffered by the savages, but to prevent them from committing the like hostilities for the future.[23]

Now returned, and once more at liberty to pursue my own inclinations, I was persuaded by my father-in-law and friends to follow some employment or other; but the plantation, from whence I was taken, tho' an exceeding good one, could not tempt me to settle on it again. What my fate would have been if I had may easily be conceived. And there being at this time (as the assembly too late for many of us found) a necessity for raising men to check those barbarians in their ravaging depredations, I inlisted myself as one with the greatest alacrity and most determined resolution, to exert the utmost of my power, in being revenged on the hellish authors of my ruin. General *Shirly* governor of *New-England*, and commander in chief of his majesty's land forces in *North America*, was pitched upon, to direct the operations of the war, in that part of the world.[24]

Into a regiment, immediately under the command of this general, was it my lot to be placed for three years. This regiment was intended for the frontiers, to destroy the forts erected by the *French*, as soon as it should be completely furnished with arms, &c. at *Boston* in *New-England*, where it was ordered for that purpose. Being then very weak, and infirm in the body, tho' possessed of my resolution, it was thought adviseable to leave me for two months in winter-quarters. At the end of which, being pretty well recruited in strength, I set out for *Boston*, to join the regiment with some others, likewise left behind; and after crossing the river *Delaware*, we arrived at *New-Jersey*, and from thence proceeded thro' the same by *New-York*, *Middletown*, *Mendon* in *Connecticut*, to *Boston*, where we arrived about the end of *March*, and found the regiment ready to receive us.

Boston, being the capital of *New-England*, and the largest city in *America*, except two or three on the *Spanish* continent, I shall here subjoin a short account of it.

'Tis pleasantly situated, and about four miles in compass, at the bottom of *Massachuset's* bay, into which there is but one common and safe passage, and not very broad, there being scarce room for three ships to come in a breast; but once in, there's room for the anchorage of 500 sail. It is guarded by several rocks, and above a dozen islands; the most remarkable of these islands is *Castle-Island*, which stands about a league from the town, and so situated, that no ship of burthen can approach the town, without the hazard of being shattered in pieces by its cannon. It is now called *Fort-William*, and mounted with 100 pieces of ordnance; 200 more which were given to the province by Queen *Anne*, are placed on a plat-form, so as to rake a ship fore and aft, before she can bring about her broadsides to bear against the castle. Some of these cannon are 42 pounders; 500 able men are exempted from all military duty in times of war, to be ready at an hour's warning, to attend the service of the castle, upon a signal of the approach of an enemy, which there seems to be no great danger of at *Boston*; where, in 24 hour's time, 10,000 effective men, well arm'd might be ready for their defence. According to a computation of the collectors of the *Light-house*, it appear'd there were 24,000 tons of shipping cleared annually.

The pier is at the bottom of the bay, 2000 feet long, and runs so far into the bay, that ships of the greatest burthen may unload without the help of boats or lighters. At the upper end of the chief street in the town, which comes down to the head of the pier, is the *Town-house*, or *Exchange*, a fine building, containing, besides the walk for merchants, the *Council chamber*, the *House of Commons*, and a spacious room for the courts of justice. The *Exchange* is surrounded with booksellers shops that have a good trade: Here being five printing houses, and the presses generally full of work, which is in a great measure owing to the colleges and schools in *New-England*; and likewise at *New-York* and *Philadelphia*, there are several printing-houses lately erected, and booksellers constantly employed, as well as at *Virginia, Maryland, South-Carolina, Barbadoes*, and the *Sugar-Islands*.

The town lies in the form of an half-moon round the harbour, and consisting of about 4000 houses, must make an agreeable prospect; the surrounding shore being high, the streets long, and the buildings beautiful. The pavement is kept in so good order, that to gallop an horse on it is 3s. 4d. forfeit. The number of inhabitants is computed at about 24,000.

There are eight churches, the chief of which is called the *Church of England church*; besides the *Baptist* meeting, and the *Quakers* meeting.

The conversation in this town is as polite as in most of the cities and towns in *England*. A gentleman of *London* would fancy himself at home at *Boston*, when he observes the number of people, their furniture, their tables, and dress, which perhaps, is as splendid as showy as that of most tradesmen in *London*.[25]

In this city, learning military discipline, and wanting for an opportunity of carrying our schemes into execution, we lay till the first of *July*; during all which time great outrages and devastations were committed by the savages in the back parts of the province. One instance of which, in particular, I shall relate, as being concerned in rewarding, according to desert, the wicked authors thereof.

Joseph Long, Esq; a gentleman of large fortune in these parts, who had in his time been a great warrior among the *Indians*, and frequently joined in expeditions with those in our interest, against the others. His many exploits, and great influence among several of the nations, were too well known to pass unavenged by the savages against whom he had exerted his abilities. Accordingly, in *April* 1756, a body of them came down on his plantation, about 30 miles from *Boston*, and skulking in the woods for some time, at last seized an opportunity to attack his house, in which, unhappily proving successful, they scalped, mangled, and cut to pieces, the unfortunate gentleman, his wife, and nine servants; and then made a general conflagration of his houses, barns, cattle, and every thing he possessed, which, with the mangled bodies, were all consumed in one blaze! But his more unfortunate son and daughter were made prisoners, and carried off by them, to be reserved for greater tortures. Alarmed and terrified at this inhuman butchery, the neighbourhood, as well as the people of *Boston*, quickly assembled themselves, to think of proper measures to be revenged on these execrable monsters. Among the first of those, who offered themselves to go against the savages, was *James Crawford*, Esq; who was then at *Boston*, and heard of this tragedy; he was a young gentleman who had for some years, paid his addresses to Miss *Long*, and was in a very little time to have been married to her. Distracted, raving, and shocked as he was, he lost no time, but instantly raised an hundred resolute and bold young fellows, to go in quest of the villains. As I had been so long among them, and was pretty well acquainted with their manners and customs, and particularly their skulking-places in the woods, I was recommended to him as one proper for his expedition; he immediately applied to my officers and got liberty for me.

Never did I go on any enterprize with half that alacrity and chearfulness I now went with this party. My wrongs and sufferings were too recent in my memory, to suffer me to hesitate a moment in taking an opportunity of being revenged to the utmost of my power.

Being quickly armed and provided, we hastened forwards for Mr. *Long's* plantation on the 29th, and after travelling the most remote and intricate paths through the woods, arrived there the 2d of *May*, dubious of our success, and almost despairing of meeting with the savages, as we had heard or could discover nothing of them in our march. In the afternoon, some of our men being sent to the top of a hill to look out for them, soon perceived a great smoak in a part of the low grounds. This we immediately, and rightly conjectured to proceed from a fire made by them. We accordingly put ourselves into regular order, and marched forwards, resolving, let their number have been what it might, to give them battle.

Arriving within a mile of the place, captain *Crawford*; whose anxiety and pain, made him quicker sighted than any of the rest, soon perceived them, and guessed their number to be about 50. Upon this we halted, and secreted ourselves as well as we could, till twelve o'clock at night. At which time, supposing them to be at rest, we divided out men into two divisions, 50 in each, and marched on; when coming within twenty yards of them, the captain fired his gun, which was immediately followed by both divisions in succession, who instantly rushing on them with bayonets fixed, killed every man of them.

Great as our joy was, and flushed with success as we were at this sudden victory, no heart among us but was ready to burst at the sight of the unhappy young lady. What must the thoughts, torments, and sensations of our brave captain then be, if even we who knew her not, were so sensibly affected! For, oh! What breast, tho' of the brutal savage race we had just destroyed, could, without feeling the most exquisite grief and pain, behold in such infernal power, a lady in the bloom of youth, blest with every female accomplishment that could set off the most exquisite beauty! Beauty, which rendered her the envy of her own sex, and the delight of ours, enduring the severity of a windy, rainy night! Behold one nurtured in the most tender manner, and by the most indulgent parents, quite naked, and in the open woods, encircling with her alabaster arms and hands a cold rough tree, whereto she was bound, with cords so straitly pull'd, that the blood trickled from her finger's ends! Her lovely tender body and delicate limbs, cut, bruised, and torn with stones, and boughs of trees as she had been dragged along, and all besmeared with blood! What heart can even now, unmoved, think of her destress, in such a deplorable condition; having no creature, with the least sensations of humanity, near to succour or relieve her, or even pity or regard her flowing tears and lamentable wailings!

The very remembrance of the sight, has at this instant such an effect upon me, that I almost want words to go on. Such then was the condition in which we found this wretched fair, but faint and speechless with the shock our firing had given her tender frame. The captain for a long time could do nothing but gaze upon and clasp her to his bosom, crying, raving, and tearing his hair like one bereft of his senses; nor did he for some time perceive the lifeless condition she was in, until one of the men had untied her lovely mangled arms, and she fell to the ground. Finding among the villains plunder the unhappy lady's cloaths, he gently put some of them about her; and after various trials and much time spent, recovered her dissipated spirits, the repossession of which she first manifested by eagerly fixing her eyes on her dear deliverer, and smiling with the most complaisant joy, blessed the Almighty, and him, for her miraculous deliverance.

During this pleasing, painful interview, our men were busily employed in cutting, hacking and scalping the dead *Indians*; and so desirous was every man to have a share in wreaking his revenge on them, that disputes happened among ourselves who should be the instruments of further shewing it on their lifeless trunks, there not being enough for every man to have one wherewith to satiate himself: The captain observing the animosity between us on this occasion, ordered, that the two divisions should cast lots for this bloody, though agreeable piece of work: which being accordingly done, the party, whose lot it was to be excluded from this business, stood by with half-pleased countenances, looking on the rest; who with the utmost cheerfulness and activity pursued their revenge in scalping, and otherwise treating their dead bodies as the most inveterate hatred and detestation could suggest.

The work being done, we thought of steering homewards triumphant with the 50 scalps; but how to get the lady forwards, who was in such a condition as rendered her incapable of walking further, gave us some pain, and retarded us a little, until we made a sort of carriage to seat her on; and then, with the greatest readiness, we took our turns, four at a time, and carried her along. This in some measure, made the captain chearful, who all the way endeavoured to comfort and revive his desponding afflicted mistress: but alas! in vain; for the miseries she had lately felt, and the terrible fate of her poor brother, of whom, I doubt not but the tender-hearted reader is anxious to hear, rendered even her most pleasing thoughts, notwithstanding his soothing words, corroding and insufferable.

The account she gave of their disastrous fate and dire catastrophe, besides what I have already mentioned, was, that the savages had no sooner seen all consumed, but they hurried off with her and her brother, pushing, and sometimes dragging them on, for four or five miles, when they stopt; and stripping her naked, treated her in a shocking manner, whilst others were stripping and cruelly whipping her unhappy brother. After which, they in the same manner pursued their journey, regardless of the tears, prayers, or intreaties of this wretched pair; but with the most infernal pleasure, laughed and rejoiced at the calamities and distresses they had brought them to, and saw them suffer, until they arrived at the place we found them; where, they had that day butchered her beloved brother in the following execrable and cruel manner: They first scalped him alive, and after mocking his agonizing groans and torments, for some hours, ripped open his belly, into which they put splinters, and chips of pine-trees, and set fire thereto; the same (on account of the turpentine wherewith these trees abound) burnt with great quickness and fury for a little time, during which, he remained in a manner alive, as she could sometimes perceive him to move his head, and groan. They then piled a great quantity of wood all round his body, and consumed it to ashes.

Thus did these Barbarians put an end to the being of this unhappy young gentleman, who was only 22 years of age when he met his calamitous fate. She continued her relation, by acquainting us, that the next day was to have seen her perish in the like manner, after suffering worse than even such a terrible death, the satisfying these diabolical miscreants in their brutal lust. But it pleased the Almighty to permit us to rescue her, and intirely extirpate this crew of devils!

Marching easily on her account, we returned to the captain's plantation the 6th of *May*, where, as well as at *Boston*, we were joyfully received, and rewarded handsomely for the scalps of those savages we had brought with us. Mr. *Crawford* and Miss *Long* were soon after married; and, in gratitude to the services we had done them, the whole party were invited to the wedding, and nobly entertained, but no riotous or noisy mirth was allowed, the young lady, as we may well imagine, being still under great affliction, and in a weak state of health.[26]

Nothing further material, that I now remember, happened during my stay at *Boston*; to proceed therefore, with the continuation of our intended expedition.

On the 1st of *July*, the regiment began their march for *Oswego*[27]. The 21st we arrived at *Albany*, in *New-York*, through *Cambridge*, *Northampton*, and *Hadfield*, in *New-England*. From thence, marching about twenty miles farther, we encamped near the mouth of the *Mohawk* river by a town called *Schenectady*, not far from the *Endless-Mountains*[28]. Here did we lye some time, until *Batteaux* (a sort of flat-bottomed boats, very small, and sharp at both ends) could be got to carry our stores and provisions to *Oswego*; each of which, would contain about six barrels of Pork, or in proportion thereto. Two men belonged to every batteaux, who made use of strong scutting poles, with iron at the ends, to prevent their being too soon destroyed by the stones in the river (one of the sources of the *Ohio*[29]) which abounded with many, and large ones, and in some places was so shallow that the men were forced to wade and drag their batteaux after them. Which, together with some Cataracts, or great falls of water, rendered this duty very hard and fatiguing, not being able to travel more than seven or eight English miles a day, until they came to the *Great-Carrying* place at *Wood's Creek*, where the provisions and batteaux were taken out, and carried about four miles to *Alliganey*, or *Ohio* great river, that runs quite to *Oswego*[30], to which place, general Shirley got with part of the forces on the 8th of *August*; but Colonel *Mercer*[31] with the remainder, did not arrive untill the 31st. Here we found Colonel *Schuyler*[32] with his regiment of *New-Jersey* provincials, who had arrived there some time before. A short description of a place, which has afforded so much occasion for animadversion, may not here be altogether disagreeable to those unacquainted with our settlements in that part of the world.

Oswego is situated N. Lat. 43 deg. 20 min. near the mouth of the river *Onondago*,[33] on the south-side of the lake *Ontario*, or *Cataraquie*. There was generally a fort and constant garrison of regular troops kept before our arrival. In the proper seasons a fair for the *Indian* trade is kept here: *Indians* of above twenty different nations have been observed here at a time. The greatest part of the trade between *Canada* and the *Indians*, of the *Great Lakes*, and some parts of the *Mississippi*, pass near this fort; the nearest and safest way of carrying goods upon this lake being along the south-side of it. The distance from *Albany* to *Oswego* fort is about 300 miles[34] west; to render which march more comfortable, we met with many good farms and settlements by the way. The *Outawaes* [Ottawas] a great and powerful nation, living upon the *Outawae* river, which joins the *Catarique* river[35], (the out-let of the great lake) deal considerably with the *New-York* trading houses here.

The different nations trading to *Oswego* are distinguishable by the variety and different fashions of their canoes; the very remote *Indians* are cloathed in skins of various sorts, and have all fire-arms: some come so far north as *Port-Nelson*, in *Hudson's* Bay, N. lat. 57 deg. And some from the *Chirakees* west of *South-Carolina*, in N. lat. 32 deg. This seems indeed to be a vast extent of in-land water-carriage, but it is only for canoes, and the smallest of craft.

Nor will it in this place be improper to give some account of our friends in those parts, whom we call the *Mohawks*, viz. The *Iroquois*, commonly called the *Mohawks*; the *Oneiadaes* [Oneidas], the *Onondagues* [Onondagas], the *Cayugaes* [Cayugas], and the *Senekeas* [Senecas]. In all accounts they are lately called the *Six Nations* of the *New-York*, friendly-*Indians*; the *Tuscararoes* [Tuscaroras], stragglers from the old *Tuscararoes* of *North-Carolina*, lately are reckoned as the sixth. I shall here reckon them as I have been informed they were formerly. 1. The *Mohawks*; they live upon the *Mohawk's* or *Schenectady* river, and head, or lye north of *New-York, Pensylvania, Maryland,* and some part of *Virginia*; having a castle or village, westward from *Albany* forty miles, and another sixty-five miles west, and about 160 sensible men. 2. The *Oneiadaes*, about eighty miles from the *Mohawk's* second village, consisting of about near 200 fighting men. 3. The *Onondagues*, about twenty-five miles further, (the famous *Oswego* trading place on the lake *Ontario*, is in their country) consisting of about 250 men. 4. The *Cayugaes*, about seventy miles further, of about 130 men; and, 5. The *Senekeas*, who reach a great way down the river *Sesquehana*, consist of about 700 marching, fighting men: so that the fighting men of the five or six nations of *Mohawks* may be reckoned at 1500 men, and extend from *Albany*, west 400 miles, lying in about thirty tribes or governments. Besides these, there is settled above *Montreal*, which lies N.E. of *Oswego*, a tribe of scoundrel run-aways from the *Mohawks*; they are called *Kahnuages* [Kahnawakes], consisting of about eighty men. This short account of these nations, I think necessary to make the *English* reader acquainted with, as I may have occasion to mention things concerning some of them.

It may not be improper here also, to give a succinct detail, of the education, manners, religion, &c. of the natives. The *Indians* are born tolerably white; but they take a great deal of pains to darken their complexion, by anointing themselves with grease, and lying in the sun. Their features are good, especially those of the women. Their limbs clean, straight, and well-proportiond, and a crooked and deformed person is a great rarity among them. They are very ingenious in their way, being neither so ignorant, nor so innocent, as some people imagine: On the contrary, a very understanding generation are they, quick of apprehension, sudden in dispatch, subtle in their dealings, exquisite in their inventions, and in labour assiduous: The world has no better marksmen with guns, or bows and arrows, than the natives, who can kill birds flying, fishes swimming, and wild beasts running; nay with such prodigious force do they discharge their arrow, that one of them will shoot a man quite through, and nail both of his arms to his body with the same arrow.

As to their religion, in order to reconcile the different accounts exhibited by travellers, we must suppose that different tribes may have different notions, and different rites: and though I do not think myself capable of determining the case with the precision and accuracy I could wish; yet, with what I have collected from my own observation when among them, and the information of my brother captives, who have been longer conversant with the *Indians* than I was; I shall readily give the public all the satisfaction I can.

Some assure us the *Indians* worship the images of some inferior deities, whose anger they seem to dread: on which account the generality of our travellers denominate the objects of their devotion, devils; though at the same time, it is allowed they pray to their inferior deities for success in all their undertakings, for plenty of food and other necessaries of life. It appears too, that they acknowledge one Supreme Being, but him they adore not, because they believe he is too far exalted above them, and too happy in himself to be concerned about the trifling affairs of poor mortals. They seem also to believe a future state, and that, after death, they will be removed to their friends who have gone before them to an *Elysium* or *Paradise* beyond the *Western Mountains*: others again, allow them either no religion at all, or, at most, very faint ideas of a deity; but all agree that they are extravagantly superstitious, and exceedingly afraid of evil spirits. To these *Demons* they make oblations every new-moon, for the space of seven days; during which time, they cast lots, and sacrifice one of themselves, putting the person devoted to the most exquisite misery they can invent, in order to satisfy the devil for that moon; for they think if they please but the evil spirit, God will do them no hurt.

Certain however it is, that those *Indians*, whom the *French* priests have had an opportunity of ministering unto, are induced to believe, "That the Son of God came into the world to save all mankind, and destroy all evil spirits that now trouble them; that the English have killed him; and that ever since, the evil spirits are permitted to walk on the earth: that if the *English* were, all destroyed, the Son of the Good-man, who is God, would come again, and banish all evil spirits from their lands, and then they would have nothing to fear or disturb them:" Cajoled by these false but artful insinuations of the *French Jesuits*, the *Indians* from that time, have endeavoured to massacre all the *English*, in order that the Son of God might come again on the earth, and rid them from their slavish fears and terrible apprehensions, by exterminating the objects thereof.

Being now at *Oswego*, the principal object that gave at that time any concern to the *Americans*, I shall, before I continue my own account, give a short recital of what had been done in these parts, in regard to the defence and preservation of the fort and the colonies thereabouts, before I came, upon such authorities as I got from those who had been long at *Oswego*, and I can well depend upon for truth.

General *Shirley*, in 1754, having erected two new forts on the river *Onondoga*[36], it seemed probable, that he intended to winter at *Oswego* with his army, that he might the more readily proceed to action in the ensuing spring. What produced his inactivity afterwards, and how it was, that fort *Oswego* was not taken by the *French* in the spring of 1755, are things my penetration will not enable me to discuss. But *Oswego* is now lost, and would have been so in the spring of 1755, if more important affairs had not made the *French* neglect it. At this time the garrison of *Oswego* consisted only of 100 men, under captain *King*[37]. The old fort being their only protection, which mounted only eight four pounders, was incapable of defence, because it was commanded by an eminence directly cross a narrow river, the banks of which were covered with thick wood.

In *May* 1755, *Oswego* being in this condition, and thus garrisoned; thirty *French* batteaux were seen to pass, and two days after eleven more; each batteaux (being much larger than ours) containing fifteen men: so this fleet consisted of near 600 men: A force, which, with a single mortar, might soon have taken possession of the place.

A resolution was now taken to make the fort larger, and erect some new ones; to build vessels upon the lake; to increase the garrison; and provide every thing necessary to annoy the enemy, so as they might render the place tenable. Captain *Broadstreet*[38] arriving on the 27th of *May* at the fort, with two companies, some small swivil guns, and the first parcel of workmen, made some imagine that a stop would be put to the *French* in their carrying men in sight of the garrison; yet, they still permitted eleven more *French* batteaux to pass by, tho' we were then superior to them in these boats, or at least in number. The reason our forces *could not* attack them, was, because they were four miles in the Offing, on board large vessels, in which the soldiers could stand to fire without being overset; and our batteaux, in which we must have attacked them, were so small, that they would contain only six men each, and so ticklish, that the inadvertent motion of one man would overset them. No care, however, was taken to provide larger boats against another emergency of the same kind. At *Oswego*, indeed, it was impracticable for want of *iron-work*; such being the provident forecast of those who had the management of affairs, that thought there were smiths enough, yet, there was, at this place, but one pair of bellows, so that the first accident that should happen to that necessary instrument, would stop all the operations of the forge at once.

The beginning of *June*, the ship-carpenters arrived from *Boston*, and on the 28th of the same month, the first vessel we ever had on the lake *Ontario*, was launched and fitted out: She was a schooner 40 feet in the keel, had 14 oars, and 12 swivel guns. This vessel, and 320 men, was all the force we had at *Oswego*, the beginning of *July*, and was victualled at the expence of the province of *New-York*. Happy indeed, it was, that the colony provisions were there; for so little care had been taken to get the king's provisions sent up, that, when we arrived, we must have perished with famine, had we not found a supply, which we had little reason to expect.

About the middle of *July*, an attack was again expected, when we (the forces under general *Shirly*) were still near 300 miles distant. And, if the attack had then been made, with the force the enemy was known to have had at hand, it must, for the reason I have just before given, have fallen into their possession.

Such was the state of *Oswego*, when we arrived there: Where we had been but a small time, before provisions began to be very scarce; and the king's allowance being still delayed, the provincial stores were soon exhausted, and we were in danger of being soon famished, being on less than half allowance. The men being likewise worn out, and fatigued with the long march they had suffered, and being without rum (or allowed none at least) and other proper nutriment, many fell sick of the flux[39], and died; so that our regiment was greatly reduced in six weeks time: A party that we left at the important carrying-place, at *Wood's creek*, being absolutely obliged to desert it for want of necessaries.

Sickness, death and desertion, had at length so far reduced us, that we had scarce men enough to perform duty, and protect those that were daily at work. The *Indians* keeping a strict look-out, rendered every one who passed the out-guards or centinels in danger of being scalped or murdered. To prevent consequences like these, a captain's guard of sixty men, with two lieutenants, two serjeants, two corporals, and one drum, besides two flank-guards of a serjeant, corporal, and twelve men in each, were daily mounted, and did duty as well as able. Scouting parties were likewise sent out every day: But the sickness still continuing, and having 300 men at work, we were obliged to lessen our guards, till general *Pepperel's* regiment[40] joined us.

A little dilligence being now made use of, about the middle of *September*, four other vessels were got ready, *viz*. A decked swoop of eight guns, four pounders, and 30 swivils; a decked schooner, eight guns, four pounders, and twenty eight swivils; one undecked schooner, of fourteen swivils, and fourteen oars, and another of twelve swivils; and fourteen oars; about 150 tons each.

On the 24th of *October*, with this armament, and a considerable number of batteaux, which were too small to live upon the lake in moderate weather, we were preparing to attack *Niagara*[41]; tho' (notwithstanding we had taken all the provisions we could find in *Oswego*, and had left the garrison behind, with scarce enough for three days) the fleet had not provisions sufficient on board, to carry them within sight of the enemy, and supplies were not to be got, within 300 miles of the place we were going against. However, the impracticability of succeeding in an expedition, undertaken without victuals, was discovered [in] time enough to prevent our march, or embarkation, or whatever it may be called; but not before nine batteaux laden with officers baggage, were sent forwards, four men in each batteau; in one of which, it was my lot to be. The men being weak, and in low spirits, with continual harassing, and low feeding, rendered our progress very tedious and difficult; add to this the places we had to pass and ascend; for, in many parts, the *Cataracts* or *falls* of water, which descended near the head of the river *Onondaga* (in some places near 100 feet perpendicular) rendered it almost impossible for us to proceed; for the current running from the bottom, was so rapid, that the efforts of twenty or thirty men were sometimes required to drag the boats along, and especially to get them up the hills or *Cataracts*, which we were forced to do with ropes: Sometimes, when with great labour and difficulty, we had got them up, we carried them by land near a quarter of a mile, before we came to any water. In short, we found four men to a batteau insufficient; for the men belonging to one batteau were so fatigued and worn out, that they could not manage her, so that the[y] lay behind almost a league.

The captain that was with us, observing this, as soon as we had got the others over the most difficult falls, ordered two besides myself to go and help her forwards; Accordingly I got into her in order to steer her, whilst my two comrades and her own crew dragged her along. When we got to any *Cataracts*, I remained in her to fasten the ropes, and keep all safe, while they hauled her up; but drawing her to the summit of the last *Cataract*, the ropes gave way, and down she fell, into a very rapid and boisterous stream; where, not being able by myself, to work her, she stove to pieces on a small rock, on which some part of her remaining till morning I miraculously saved myself. Never was my life in greater danger than in this situation; the night being quite dark, and no assistance to be obtained from any of my comrades; tho' many of them, as I afterwards learned, made diligent search for me; but the fall of the water rendered the noise that they, as well as myself made, to be heard by one another, quite ineffectual.

In the morning, they indeed found me, but in a wretched condition, quite benumbed, and almost dead with cold, having nothing on but my shirt.

After various efforts, having with great difficulty got me up, they used all proper means to recover my worn-out spirits; but the fire had a fatal effect to what they intended, for my flesh swelled all over my body and limbs, and caused such a deprivation of my senses, that I fainted, and was thought by all to be dead. However, after some time, they pretty well recovered my scattered senses, and fatigued body; and with proper care conducted me with some others (who were weak and ill of the flux) to *Albany*, where the hospital received our poor debilitated bodies.

The rest, not able to proceed, or being countermanded, bent their course back again to *Oswego*: Where, a friendly storm preventing an embarkation, when a stock of provisions was got together (sufficient to prevent them from eating one another, during the first twelve days) all thoughts of attacking *Niagara* were laid aside.

Thus ended this formidable campaign. The vessels that we had built (as I afterwards learned) were unrigged and laid up, without having been put to any use; while a *French* vessel was cruising on the *Lake*, and carrying supplies to *Niagara*, without interruption; five others as large as ours being also ready to launch at *Frontenac*[42], which lays across the lake *Ontario*, north of *Oswego*.

The general [Shirley], whatever appearances might have led others, as well as myself, to think otherwise, soon indicated his intention of not wintering at *Oswego*; for he left the place before the additional works were compleated, and the garrison, by insensible degrees, decreased to 1100 men; still living in perpetual terror, on the brink of famine, and become mutinous for want of their pay; which, in the *hurry of military business*, during a year that was crowned with great events, had been forgotten: for, from my first inlisting, to the time I was laid up at *Albany*, I never had received above six weeks pay.

A little, indeed, may be offered in vindication of the general in regard to the numberless delays of this campaign, *viz*. That it took some time to raise the two regiments which were in *British* pay, as the name of enlisting for life, is somewhat forbidding to the *Americans*: (a few of whom, as well as myself, made our agreement for three years; but after that time, I doubt, we must have depended on his pleasure for our being discharged, according to our contract, had it not fallen out otherwise).

The unusual dryness of the summer, rendered the rivers down to *Oswego* in some places impassable; or very difficult for the batteaux to proceed; and it was whispered, that a gentleman, lately in an eminent station in *New-York*, did all in his power to hinder the undertaking, from a pique to the general.[43] By these disadvantages, he was detained at *Albany*, till August, and even when he did reach *Oswego*, he found himself put to no little difficulty to maintain his ground for want of provisions; and the men being so reduced, more than once, to short allowance, as you have seen, became troubled with the flux, and had not any thing necessary, not even rum sufficient for the *common* men, to prevent the fatal effects of that disorder.

In this manner, the summer was spent on our side; and the reason why the *French* did not this year take *Oswego*, when they might, with so little trouble, was, as many besides myself conjectured, that they thought it more their interest, to pursue their projects on the *Ohio*, and preserve the friendship of the considerable *Indians*; which an attack upon *Oswego*, at that time, would have destroyed.

How far they succeeded in such their projects, and the reasons of their successes, a little animadversion of our own transactions will let us into the light of. For, as appearances on our side were very favourable in the spring; general *Braddock's* defeat greatly increased the gloom, which sat on the countenances of the *Americans*.

Great things being expected from him, he arrived early in the spring at *Virginia*, with a considerable land force; and fort *Du Quesne* seemed to be ours, if we did but go and demand it. The attacks designed against *Niagara*, and fort *Frederick*, at *Crown-point*[44], were planned in the winter, and the troops employed against the *French* in *Nova-Scotia*, embarked at *Boston* in *April*. Let us view the events besides those already mentioned. General *Braddock* was ready to march in *April*. But through ignorance, or neglect, or a misunderstanding with the governor of *Virginia*, had neither fresh provisions, horses, nor waggons provided; and so late as the latter end of *May*, it was necessary to apply to *Pensylvania*, for the most part of those. This neglect created a most pernicious diffidence and discredit of the *Americans*, in the mind of the general, and prevented their usefulness, where their advice was wanted, and produced very bad effects. He was a man (as it is now too well known and believed) by no means of quick apprehension, and could not conceive that such people could instruct him; and his young counsellors prejudiced him still more, so as to slight his officers, and what was worse, his enemy; as it was treated as an absurdity to suppose the *Indians* would ever attack regulars: And of course, no care was taken to instruct the men, to resist their peculiar manner of fighting. Had this circumstance been attended to, I am fully persuaded, 400 *Indians*, about the number that defeated him, would have given him very little annoyance: Sure I am, 400 of our people, rightly managed, would have made no difficulty of driving before them four times that handful, to whom he owed his defeat and death.

The undertaking of the eastern provinces to reduce the fort at *Crown-Point*[45], met that fate, which the jarring counsels of a divided people commonly meet with; for though the plan was concerted in the winter of 1754, it was *August* before these petty governments could bring together their troops. In short, it must be owned by all, that delays were the banes of our undertakings, except in the bay of *Fundi*, in *Nova-Scotia*, where secrecy and expedition were rewarded with success, and that province reduced.[46]

The general continued inactive, from the time [he] left *Oswego*, to *March* 1756, when he was about to resume the execution of his scheme to attack *Frontenac* and *Niagara*. What would have been the issue of this project, neither myself, nor any other person, can now pretend to say, for, just at this crisis, he received orders from *England*, to attempt nothing, till lord *Loudon*[47] should arrive, which was said should be early in the spring. However, his lordship did not get there untill the middle of *July*, so that by this delay, time was given to the marquis *de Montcalm* (major general *Dieskau's* successor)[48] to arrive from *France* at *Canada* with 3000 regular forces, and take the field before us.

But to return from this digression to other transactions. When I was pretty well recovered again, I embarked on board a vessel from *Albany* for *New-York*; where, when I arrived, I found to my sorrow, captain *John Shirley*[49], the general's son, had been dead for some time. He was a very promising, worthy, young gentleman, and universally regretted. His company was given to major *James Kinnair*[50], who ordered that none of his men should go out on the recruiting parties, as was at first intended by his predecessor; but, that the private men should either return to *Oswego*, or do duty in the fort at *New-York*. Not liking my station here, I intreated the general, who was now arrived, for a furlow, to see my friends at *Pensylvania*, which he, having then no great occasion for me at *New-York*, granted for three months.

As I have here mentioned *New-York*, and before given a short account of the two cities, *Philadelphia* and *Boston*, it would be a disrespect shown to this elegant one not to take notice of it, as well as in some measure debarring the reader from such information, as may not be disagreeable: but not being of that note or consequence with the others, I shall briefly observe; that,

New York is a very fine city, and the capital of the province of that name; it contains about 3000 houses, and near 9000 inhabitants. The houses are all well built, and the meanest of them said to be worth 100 *l*. sterling, which cannot be said of the city of the same name, nor of any other in *England*. Their conversation is polite, and their furniture, dress, and manner of living, quite elegant. In drinking and gallantry they exceed any city in *America*.

The great church is a very handsome edifice, and built in 1695. Here is also a *Dutch* church, a *French* church, and a *Lutheran* church. The inhabitants of *Dutch* extraction, make a considerable part of the town, and most of them speak *English*.

Having obtained my furlow, I immediately set out for *Pensylvania*, and arriving at *Philadelphia*, found the consternation and terror of the inhabitants was greatly increased, to what it was when I left them. They had made several treaties of friendship with the *Indians*, who, when well supplied with arms, ammunition, clothes, and other necessaries, through the pacific measures, and defenceless state of the *Philadelphians*, soon revolted to the *French*, and committed great outrages on the back parts of the province, destroying and massacring men, women, and children, and every thing that unhappily lay in their way.

A few instances of which, together with the behaviour of the *Philadelphians* on these occasions, I shall here present the reader with, who, of whatever sect or profession, I am well assured, must condemn the pacific disposition, and private factions that then reigned, not only in the a----y [assembly], but among the magistrates themselves; who were a long time, before they could agree on proper petitions, to rouse the assembly from the lethargic and inactive condition they absolutely remained in.

For, about the middle of *October*, a large body of *Indians*, chiefly *Shawonese* [Shawnees], *Delawares*, &c. fell upon this province, from several quarters, almost at the same instant, murdering, burning, and laying waste [to] all wherever they came; so that in the five counties of *Cumberland*, *York*, *Lancaster*, *Berks*, and *Northampton*, which compose more than half the province, nothing but scenes of destruction and desolation were to be seen.

The damages which these counties had sustained by the desertion of plantations, is not to be reckoned up, nor are the miseries of the poor inhabitants to be described; many of whom, though escaping with life, were, without a moment's warning, driven from these habitations where they enjoyed every necessary of life, and were then exposed to all the severity of an hard winter, and obliged to solicit their very bread at the cold hand of charity, or perish with hunger, under the inclement air.

To these barbarities I have already mentioned, I cannot pass over the following, as introductory causes of the *Philadelphians* at last withstanding the outrages of the Barbarians.

At *Gnadenhutten*, a small *Moravian* settlement, in *Northampton* county[51], the poor unhappy sufferers, were sitting round their peaceful supper, when the inhuman murderers, muffled in the shades of night, dark and horrid as the infernal purposes of their diabolic souls, stole upon them, butchered, scalped them, and consumed their bodies, together with their horses, stock, and upwards of sixty head of the fat cattle, (intended for the subsistance of the brethren at *Bethlehem*[52]) all in one general flame; so that next morning furnished only a melancholy spectacle of their mingled ashes.

At the *Great Cove* in *Cumberland*, at *Tulpehockin*, in *Berks*, and in several other places[53], their barbarities were still greater, if possible. Men, women, children, and brute-beasts, shared one common destruction; and where they were not burnt to ashes, their mangled limbs were found promiscuously strewed upon the ground, those appertaining to the human form, scarce to be distinguished from the brute!

But of all the instances of the barbarities I heard of in these parts, I could not help being most affected with the following: One family, consisting of the husband, his wife and a child, only a few hours old, were all found murdered and scalped in this manner: The mother stretched on the bed, with her new born child, horibly mangled, and put under her head for a pillow, while the husband lay on the ground hard by, with his belly ript up, and his bowels laid open.

In another place, a woman with her sucking child, finding that she had fallen into the hands of the enemy, fell flat on her face, prompted by the strong call of nature, to cover and shelter her innocent child with her own body. The accursed savage rushed from his lurking place, struck her on the head with his *tomahawk*, tore off her scalp, and scoured back into the woods, without observing the child, being apprehensive that he was discovered. The child was found sometime afterwards under the body of its mother, and was then alive.

Many of their young women were carried by the savages into captivity, reserved, perhaps, for a worse fate than those who suffered death in all its horrid shapes; and no wonder, since they were reserved by savages, whose tender mercies might be accounted more cruel than their very cruelty itself.

Yet even during all this time this province (had things been properly ordered) need but, in comparison to her strength, have lifted her foot and crushed all the *French* force on their borders; but unused to such undertakings, and bound by *non-resisting principals* from exerting her strength, and involved in disputes with the proprietaries, they stood still, vainly hoping the *French* would be so moderate as to be content with their victory over *Braddock*, or at least confine their attacks to *Virginia*: But they then saw and felt all this was delusion, and the barbarities of the *Indian* parties headed by *French* officers: Notwithstanding all which they continued in domestic debates, without a soldier in pay, or a penny in the treasury. In short, if the enemy had then had but 1500 men at the *Ohio*, and would have attempted it, no rashness could have been perceived in their marching down to the city of *Philadelphia*.

Thus stood our affairs on the side of the *Ohio*, when an old captain of the warriors, in the interest of the *Philadelphians*, and their ever faithful friend, whose name was *Scarrooyda*, alias *Monokatoathy*[54], on the first notice of these misfortunes, came hastening to *Philadelphia*, together with colonel *Weiser*[55], the provincial interpreter, and two other *Indian* chiefs. *Scarrooyda* immediately demanded an audience of the assembly, who were then sitting, to whom he spoke in a very affecting manner. His speeches being printed, and sold about *Philadelphia*, I procured one of them, which was as follows.

"BRETHREN,

"We are once more come among you, and sincerely condole with you on account of the late bloodshed, and the awful cloud that hangs over you, and over us. Brethren, you may be undoubtedly assured that these horrid actions were committed by none of those nations that have any fellowship with us, but by certain falsehearted and treacherous brethren. It grieves us more than all our other misfortunes, that any of our good friends, the *English*, should suspect us of having false hearts.

"BRETHREN,

"If you were not an infatuated people, we are 300 warriors firm to your interest; and, if you are so unjust to us as to retain any doubts of our sincerity, we offer to put our wives, our children, and all we have into your hands, to deal with them as seemeth good to you, if we are found in the least to swerve from you. But, brethren, you must support and assist us, for we are not able to fight alone against the powerful nations who are coming against you; and you must this moment resolve, and give us an explicit answer what you will do: For these nations have sent to desire us, as old friends, either to join them, or get out of their way, and shift for ourselves. Alas! brethren, we are sorry to leave you! We remember the many tokens of your friendship to us: But what shall we do? We cannot stand alone, and you will not stand with us!—

"BRETHREN,
"The time is precious. While we are here consulting with you, we know not what may be the fate of our brethren at home. We do therefore once more invite and request you to act like men, and be no longer as women, pursuing weak measures that render your names despicable. If you will put the hatchet§ into our hands, and send out a number of your young men in conjunction with our warriors, and provide the necessary arms, ammunition, and provisions, and likewise build some strong houses for the protection of our old men, women and children, while we are absent in war: We shall soon wipe the tears from your eyes, and make these false hearted brethren repent their treachery and baseness towards you, and towards us.

"But we must at the same time solemnly assure you, that if you delay any longer to act in conjunction with us, or think to put us off, as usual, with uncertain hopes, you must not expect to see our faces under this roof any more. We must shift for our own saf[e]ty, and leave you to the mercy of our enemies, as an infatuated people, upon whom we can have no longer dependance."

The tears stood in the old man's eyes, while he delivered this last part; and no wonder, since the very being of his nation depended upon their joining the enemy, or our enabling them immediately to make head against them.

It was some time, however, before the assembly could be brought to consent to any vigorous measures for their own defence. Their back inhabitants lost all patience at their conduct. Until at length the governor exerted his utmost power, and procured the militia, and money bills to pass. By virtue of the former, the freemen of the province were enabled to form themselves into companies, and each company, by a majority of votes, by way of ballot, to chuse its own officers; viz. a captain, lieutenant, and ensign; who, if approved of, were to be commissioned by the governor. So that the *Philadelphians* were at last permitted to raise and arm themselves in their own defence.[56] They accordingly formed themselves into companies; the governor signing to all gentlemen qualified, who had been regularly balloted, commissions for that purpose.

§ See under the note Tomahawk, page 9.

Captain *Davis* was one of the first who had a company, and, being desirous of my service, in order to instruct the irregulars in their discipline, obtained from the governor a certificate to indemnify me from any punishment which might be adjudged by the regiment to which I already belonged: for without that I had not gone. Our company, which consisted of 100 men, was not compleated until the 24 of *December*, 1755; when, losing no time, we next morning marched from *Philadelphia* in high spirits; resolving to shew as little quarter to the savages as they had to many of us.[57]

Colonel *Armstrong* had been more expeditious, for he had raised 280 provincial irregulars, and marched a little time before against the *Ohio Morians*, but of him more hereafter.[58]

We arrived the 26th of *December* at *Bethlehem*, in the forks of the river *Delaware*, where, being kindly received by the *Moravians*, we loaded six wagons with provisions, and proceeded on to the *Appalachian Mountains*, or *Blue Hills*, to a town called *Kennorton head*[59], which the *Moravians* had deserted on account of the *Indians*. Fifty of our men, of whom I made one, were ordered before the rest, to see whether the town was destroyed or not. Disposing them to the best advantage, we marched on till we came within five miles of the place, which we found standing entire.

Having a very uneven, rugged road to it, and not above four men able to go a-breast, we were on a sudden alarmed, by the firing of the flank-guards, which were a little in the rear of our van. The savages briskly returned their fire, and killed the ensign and ten of the men, and wounded several others.

Finding this, I being chief in command (having acted as lieutenant, and received pay as such from my first entrance, for my trouble and duty in learning the company,) ordered the men to march on with all expedition to the town, and all the way to keep a running fire on the enemy, as they had fallen on our rear.

We should have got there in very good order, had it not been for a river we had to cross, and the weather being so excessively cold, our cloaths froze to our bodies as soon as we got out of the water. However, with great difficulty we reached the town, and got into the church with the loss of twenty-seven men. There we made as good preparations for our defense as possible we could, making a great fire of the benches, seats, and what we could find therein, to dry our cloaths; not esteeming it the least sacrilege or crime, upon such an emergency.

The *Indians* soon followed us into the town, and surrounding us, tried all methods to burn the church, but our continual firing kept them off for about six hours, untill our powder and ball were all expended. In the night they set several houses on fire; and we dreading the consequences of being detained there, resolved to make one bold effort, and push ourselves thro' the savages forces, which was accordingly done with the most undaunted courage. The enemy fired continually on us during our retreat, and killed many of our men, but in their confusion many of themselves also; it being so very dark that we were not well able to discern our own party; so that only five of us kept together and got into the woods; the rest whom we left behind, I doubt, fell sacrifices to the savages.

The night being so excessive cold, and having but few cloaths with us out of the church, two of my comrades froze to death, before we could reach any inhabited place. In short, we did not get any relief till four o'clock in the morning, when we arrived at a house that lay in the gap of the *Blue Hills*; where our captain had arrived with the remainder of the men and waggons the day before.[60]

The captain inquiring our success, I gave him the melancholy detail of our unfortunate expedition: upon which an express was immediately sent to the governor with the account, who ordered 1600 men to march the next morning for the same place, under the command of general *Franklin*[61], not only to bury the dead and build a fort there, but to extirpate the savages who infested these parts, and were too powerful for our small number under captain *Davis*.

The remainder of our little party were now building a fort at the place where we lay for our defence, until more assistance should arrive; for we were under continual apprehensions of the *Indians* pursuing and attacking us again.

On the 9th of *January* 1756, we were reinforced by general *Franklin* and his body; and the next day set out again for *Kennorton-head*; where, when we arrived, to our great consternation, we found little occasion to bury our unhappy comrades, the swine (which in that country are vastly numerous in the woods) having devoured their bodies, and nothing but bones strewed up and down were to be seen. We there built a fort in the place where the old church had stood, and gave it the name of fort *Allen*[62]; this was finished in six days, and in so good a manner, that 100 men would make great resistance against a much greater number of *Indians*.

On the 18th, 1400 of us were ordered about fifteen miles distant from thence, on the frontiers of the province; where we built another fort called *Fort-Norris*[63]. In our way thither we found six men scalped and murdered in a most cruel manner. By what we could discern, they had made a vigorous defence, the barrels and stocks of their guns being broke to pieces, and themselves, cut and mangled in a terrible manner.

From thence we were ordered to march towards a place called the *Minnisinkes*[64], but this journey proved longer than we were aware of. The Indians committing great outrages in these parts, having burnt and destroyed all the houses, &c. in our way: These tragic actions caused us to divide ourselves into several parties, who were ordered divers ways, to cut off as many of these savages as possible.

The day after this scheme was put into execution, we met with a small party, which we put to the rout, killing fourteen of them. We then made all possible despatch to save some houses we saw on fire, but on our nearer approach found our endeavour in vain: *John Swisher* and his family having been before scalped, and burnt to ashes in his own house. On the following night the house of *James Wallis* underwent the same fate; himself, wife, seven children, and the rest of his family, being scalped and burnt therein. The houses and families of *Philip Green* and *Abraham Nairn*, suffered in the like manner. Nor did the cruelty of these barbarians stop here, but attacked the dwelling-house of *George Hunter*, Esq; a gentleman of considerable worth, and a justice of the peace, who made a brave resistance, and rather than fall into the hands of these miscreants, chose to meet death in the flames; which he, his wife, and all his household consisting of sixteen in number, did with the utmost bravery, before any assistance could be received from our general, who had dispatched 500 of us for that purpose, on an express being sent to him that morning.[65]

From thence we marched to the *Minisinkes*, and built *Fort Norris*. On the 9th of *March* we set out with 1000 men to the head of the *Minisinkes*, and built another fort, which we named *Franklin*[66], in honour of our general. All which forts we garrisoned with as many men as we could possibly spare.

After this we were daily employed in scouring the woods from fort to fort, of these noxious creatures the *Indians*, and in getting as much of the corn together as we could find, to prevent the savages from having any benefit therefrom.

Notwithstanding our vigilance, these villains on the 15th attacked the house of *James Graham*, but by providence he, with his wife, who had just lain in, and the young infant in her arms, (with nothing about her but her shift) made their escape to *Fort Allen*, about fifteen miles distant. The child perished by the way, and it was matter of wonder to the whole garrison to find either of them alive; indeed they were in a deplorable condition, and we imagined they would expire every moment. The wife however, to our great astonishment, recovered, but the husband did not survive above six hours after their arrival.

The house of *Isaac Cook* suffered by the flames, himself, his wife, and eight children, being scalped and burnt in it.[67]

Tedious and shocking would it be to enumerate half the murders, conflagrations and outrages, committed by these hellish infidels. Let it suffice therefore, that from the year 1753, when they first began their barbarities, they had murdered, burnt, scalped, and destroyed, above 3500 souls; above 1000 whereof were unhappy inhabitants of the western part of *Philadelphia*. Men, women and children, fell alike a prey to these savages: No regard being had by them to the tender intreaties of an affectionate parent for a beloved child, or the infant's prayers in behalf of his aged father and mother. Such are the miserable calamities attendant on schemes for gratifying the ambition of a tyrannic monarch like France, or the weak contrivances and indolent measures of blundering ministers and negociators.

The time of my furlow at length expiring, I prepared to set out for my regiment. Having a recommendatory letter[68] from general *Franklin* to major *Kinnair* as to my services, I marched forward for *New York*: Where being arrived I waited on the major, he being a worthy gentleman universally beloved by the whole regiment; and after giving him an account of all our transactions, and the hardships and labours we had gone through, I was dismissed.

After some stay there, I was ordered to proceed on my march for *Oswego* once more, But before I go further with my own affairs, I shall just recount the result of those provincials, who went, as I mentioned before, to quell the savages, under the command of colonel *Armstrong*.[69]

He having under his command 280 provincials destined against the *Ohio Morians*, against whom nothing had been attempted, notwithstanding their frequent incursions and murders, penetrated 140 miles through the woods from *Fort Shirley*[70] on *Juniata* river, to *Kittanning*, an *Indian* town on the *Ohio*, about twenty-five miles above fort *Du Quesne*, belonging to the *French*. He soon joined the advanced party at the *Beaver-dams*; and, on the fourth evening, after being within six miles of *Kittanning*, the scouts discovered a fire in the road, and reported that there were but three or four *Indians* at it. At that time it was not thought proper to attempt surprising these *Indians*, lest, if one should escape, the town might be alarmed: Lieutenant *Hogg*[71] therefore, with twelve men, was left to watch them, with orders not to fall upon them until day-break; and our forces turned out of the path, to pass their fire, without disturbing them.

About three in the morning having been guided by the *whooping* of the *Indian* warriors, at a dance in the town, they reached the river at about 100 perches below it. As soon as day appeared the attack began; Captain *Jacobs*[72] chief of the *Indians*, gave the *war whoop*, and defended his house bravely through the loop-holes in the logs. The *Indians* generally refusing quarter, Colonel *Armstrong* ordered their houses to be set on fire, which was done by the officers and soldiers with great alacrity. On this some burst out of the houses and attempted to reach the river, but were instantly shot down. Captain *Jacobs* in getting out of a window was shot and scalped, as were also his *Squaw*, and a lad they called the king's son. The *Indians* had a number of spare arms in the houses loaded, which went off in quick succession as the fire came to them; and quantities of gunpowder, which had been stored in every house, blew up from time to time, throwing their bodies into the air.

Eleven *English* prisoners were released, who informed the colonel, that that very day two batteaux of *Frenchmen*, with a large party of *Delaware* and *French Indians*, were to have joined Captain *Jacobs* to march and take *Fort Shirley*; and that twenty-four warriors had set out before them the preceeding evening; which proved to be the party that had kindled the fire the preceeding night; for our people returning, found Lieutenant *Hogg* wounded in three places: and learned, that he had attacked the supposed party of three or four at the fire, but found them too strong for him. He killed three of them however, at the first fire, and fought them an hour; when, having lost three of his men, the rest, as he lay wounded, abandoned him and fled, the enemy pursuing. Lieutenant *Hogg* died soon after of his wounds.

Enough of these two expeditions has been said; nor can I well tell which of the two was most successful, both losing more of their own men, than they killed of the enemy.

A little retrospection again on the actions and behaviour of the *Philadelphians*, and the other provinces and places in conjunction with them, may here be something necessary: For, when I arrived at *Philadelphia*, I found, that however melancholy their situation had been of late, this good effect had been obtained, that the most prejudiced and ignorant individual was feelingly convinced of the necessity of vigorous measures; and, besides national and public views, then the more prevailing ones of revenge and self-interest gave a spur to their counsels. They were accordingly raising men with the utmost expedition; and had, before the end of the summer, a considerable number, though not equal to what they could furnish, having at least 45,000 men in *Pensylvania* able to fight.

And, pursuant to agreement some months before, the four governments of *New-England*, in conjunction with *New York* (which last furnished 1300) had now assembled 8000 men (for the attack of fort *Frederic*) at *Albany*, 150 miles N. of *New York*, and about 130 from *Crown-Point*, under the command of general *Winslow*.[73] But many people dreading the cruelty of the *French*, were not so very eager to join them this year as the last; an impress therefore of part of the militia was ordered in *New York* government. To prevent which, subscriptions were set on foot to engage volunteers by high bounties; so loath were they that some got nine or twelve pounds sterling to inlist.

The 44th, 48th, 50th, and 51st regiments of *Great Britain* were destined for the campaign on the great lake *Ontario*, and mostly marched for *Oswego*, thence to be carried over in 200 great whale boats, which were then at the lake, and were built at *Shenectady* on *Mohawk's* river, and were long, round and light, as the batteaux, being flat-bottomed and small, would not answer the navigation of the lake, where the waves were often very high. They were then, at last, intended to attack fort *Frontenac*, mentioned before, and the other *French* forts on the lake. Upwards of 2000 batteau men were employed to navigate the batteaux, each a ton burthen, laden with provisions and stores from *Albany* up the *Mohawk's* river, then through *Oneyda* lake and river, down to *Oswego*. There were likewise 300 sailors hired and gone up from *New-York* (as I found, when I arrived there) to navigate the four armed ships on the lake, built there, as I have before-mentioned, the last year, for the king's service, and two others were then building; smiths, carpenters, and other artifices, having gone there for that purpose some weeks before. Such were the preparations and armaments for this campaign; but how fruitless, to our great disgrace, were soon known all over the world!

I shall not trouble the reader with a long account of a long march I had to take from *New-York* to *Oswego*, to join my regiment: suffice it therefore, that I arrived there about the middle of *July*; but in my march thither with some recruits, we joined colonel *Broadstreet* at *Albany*, and on the 6th of *May*, at the *Great Carrying Place*, had a skirmish with the *French* and *Indians*, wherein several were killed and wounded on both sides; of the latter I made one. Receiving a shot through my left hand, which intirely disabled my third and fourth fingers; and having no hospital, or any conveniencies for the sick there, I was, after having my hand dressed in a wretched manner, sent with the next batteaux to *Albany* to get it cured.[74]

As soon as I was well, I set forwards for *Oswego* again. And, when arrived there, I began to make what observations I could, as to the alterations that had been made since my departure in the month of *October* preceeding. The works of *Oswego*, at this time, consisted of three forts, *viz.* The *Old Fort*, built many years before, whose chief strength was a weak stone wall, about two feet thick, so ill cemented, that it could not resist the force of a four pound ball, and situated on the east side of the harbour; the two other forts, called *Fort Ontaria* and *Fort George*, were each of them at the distance of about 450 yards from the *Old Fort*, and situated on two eminencies, which commanded it; both these, as I have already observed, were begun to be built last year upon plans, which made them defensible against musquetry, and cannon of three or four pound ball only; the time not allowing works of a stronger nature to be then undertaken.

For our defense against large cannon, we entirely depended on a superior naval force upon the lake, which might have put it in our power to prevent the *French* from bringing heavy artillery against the place, as that could only be done by water-carriage, which is my opinion, as well as many others. If the naval force had but done their duty, *Oswego* might have been ours to this very day, and intirely cut off the communication of the *French* from *Canada* to the *Ohio*: But if I would insist on this, as the particulars require, I perhaps should affront some, and injure myself, all to no purpose or of any beneficial service to recall our former losses; for that reason, I shall deter enlarging on the subject, although, at the same time, I can give very good circumstances to maintain my argument, if required.

A day or two after being at *Oswego*, the fort was alarmed by hearing a firing; when on dispatching proper scouts, it was found to be the *French* and *Indians* engaging the batteau-men and sailors, convoying the provisions of *Oswego*, from one river to another. On this a detachment of 500 men were ordered out in pursuit of them, whereof I was one. We had a narrow pass in the woods to go through, where we were attacked by a great number of *Indians*, when a desperate fight began on both sides, that lasted about two hours. However, at last we gained a complete victory, and put them intirely to the rout, killing fourteen of them, and wounding about forty. On our side we had but two men killed and six wounded. Many more would have been killed of both parties, had it not been for the thickness of the woods.

I cannot here omit recounting a most singular transaction that happened during this my second time of being there, which, though scarce credible, is absolutely true, and can be testified by hundreds, who know, and have often seen the man; in short, one *Moglasky* of the 50th regiment, an *Irishman*, being placed as centinel over the rum which had arrived, and being curious to know its goodness, pierced the cask, and drank till he was quite intoxicated; when, not knowing what he did, he rambled from his post, and fell asleep a good way from the garrison. An *Indian* skulking that way for prey, (as is conjectured) found him, and made free with his scalp, which he plucked and carried off. The serjeant in the morning, finding him prostrate on his face, and seeing his scalp off, imagined him to be dead; but on his nearer approach, and raising him from the ground, the fellow awaked from the sound sleep he had been in, and asked the serjeant what he wanted. The serjeant, quite surprised at the strange behavior of the fellow, interrogated him, how he came there in that condition? He replied, *He could not tell; but that he had got very drunk, and rambled he knew not whither.* The serjeant advised him to prepare for death, not having many hours to live, as he had lost his scalp. *Arrah, my dear, now* (cries he) *and are you joking me?* for he really knew nothing of his being served in the manner he was, and would not believe any accident had happened him, until feeling his clothes bloody, he felt his head, and found it to be too true, as well as having a cut from his mouth to his ear. He was immediately carried before the governor, who asking him, how he came to leave his post? He replied, *That being very thirsty, he had broached a cask of rum, and drank about a pint, which made him drunk; but if his honour would forgive him, he'd never be guilty of the like again.* The governor told him, it was very probably he never would, as he was now no better than a dead man. However, the surgeons dressed his head there, as well as they could, and then sent him in a batteau to *Albany*, where he was perfectly cured; and to the great surprise of every body, was living when I left the country. This, though so extraordinary and unparalleled an affair, I aver to be true; having several times seen the man after this accident happened to him. How his life was preserved seems a miracle, as no instance of the like was ever known.[75]

I had forgot to mention, That before I left *Albany* the last time, upon colonel *Broadstreet*'s arrival there, in his way to *Oswego*, with the provisions and forces, consisting of about 500 whale boats and batteaux, intended for the campaign on the great lake *Ontario*, mentioned before; I joined his corps, and proceeded on with the batteaux, &c.

Going up the river *Onondaga* towards *Oswego*, the batteau-men were on the 29th of *June*, attacked near the *Falls*, about nine miles from *Oswego*, by 500 *French* and *Indians*, who killed and wounded 74 of our men, before we could get on shore, which, as soon as we did, the *French* were routed, with the loss of 130 men killed, and several wounded, whom we took prisoners.

Had we known of their lying in ambush, or of their intent to attack us, the victory would have been much more compleat on our side, as the troops colonel *Broadstreet* commanded, were regular, well disciplined, and in tolerable health, whereas the *French*, by a long passage at sea and living hard after their arrival at *Canada*, were much harrassed and fatigued.

However, we got all safe to *Oswego* with the batteaux and provisions, together with rigging and stores for the large vessels, excepting twenty four cannon, six pounders, that were then at the *Great Carrying-Place*; which colonel *Broadstreet* was to bring with him, upon his next passage, from *Schenectady*; to which place, as soon as he had delivered to the quarter-master all the stores under his care, he was ordered to return with the batteaux and men to receive the orders of major-general *Abercrombie*[76]. In his return from Schenectady, it was expected that *Halket*'s and *Dunbar*'s regiments[77] would have come with him, in order to take fort *Frontenac*, and the other *French* forts on the lake *Ontario*. But, alas! as schemes for building castles in the air always prove abortive, for want of proper architecture and foundation, so did this scheme of ours, for want of a due knowledge of our own situation!

On the arrival of these forces, a new brigantine and sloop were fitted out; and about the same time a large snow was also launched and rigged, and only waited for her guns and some running rigging, which they expected every day by colonel *Broadstreet*; and had he returned in time with the cannon and batteau-men under his command, the *French* would not have dared to have appeared on the lake; but colonel *Broadstreet* happened to be detained with the batteaux at *Schenectady* for above a month, waiting for the 44th regiment to march with him; The dilatoriness of this embarkation at *Schenectady* cannot be imputed to colonel *Broadstreet*, because general *Shirley* waited with impatience for the arrival of lord *Loudon Campbell* from *England*; and when his lordship landed at *New-York*, he, in a few days after, proceeded to *Albany*, where his lordship took the command of the army from general *Shirley*, and upon comparing, and considering how bad a situation his forces, and the different governments upon the continent were in, his lordship, with advice of several other experienced officers, thought himself not in a condition to proceed on any enterprize for that season, no further than to maintain our ground at *Oswego*; for which purpose, colonel *Broadstreet* was immediately ordered off with the batteaux and provisions, as also the foresaid regiments; but before *Broadstreet* arrived at the *Great Carrying-Place*, *Oswego* was taken with all the ships of war, although our naval force was far superior to the *French*.

Before I relate the attack of *Oswego*, I shall review a little what the *French* were doing during these our dilatory, pompous proceedings.

The marquis de *Vaudreuil*[78], governor and lieutenant-general of *New-France*, whilst he provided for the security of the frontiers of *Canada*, was principally attentive to the lakes. Being informed that we were making vast preparations at *Oswego* for attacking *Niagara* and *Frontenac*, he took and razed, in the month of *March*, the fort where we had formed our principal magazine, and in *June* following destroyed, on the river of *Chonegan* or *Oswego*, some of our vessels, and made some prisoners. The success of these two expeditions encouraged him to act offensively, and to attack us at *Oswego*. This settlement they pretended, and still insist on, to be an incroachment, or invasion, which we had made in a time of profound peace; and against which, they said, they had continually remonstrated, during our blundering, negotiating *Lawyer*'s residence at *France*[79]. It was at first, say they, only a fortified magazine; but in order to avail themselves of its advantageous situation in the centre almost of the *French* colonies, the *English* added, from time to time, several new works, and made it consist of three forts, as above described.

The troops designed for this expedition by the *French* amounted to near 5000 men, 1300 of which were regulars.[80] To prevent his design being discovered, M. de *Vaudreuil* pretended, in order the better to deceive us, who had so long before been blind, that he was providing only for the security of *Niagara* and *Frontenac*. The marquis de *Montcalm*, who commanded on this occasion, arrived the 29th of *July* at fort *Frontenac*; and having given the necessary directions for securing his retreat, in case it should have been rendered inevitable, by a superior force; sent out two vessels, one of twelve, and the other of sixteen guns, to cruize off *Oswego*, and posted a chain of *Canadians* and *Indians* on the road between *Oswego* and *Albany*, to intercept our couriers. All the forces, and the vessels, with the artillery and stores, being arrived in the bay of *Nixoure*[81], the place of general rendezvous, the Marquis de *Montcalm* ordered his advance guard to proceed to a creek, called *Anse aux Cabannes*, three leagues from Oswego. But,

To carry on this account the more accurate and intelligible to the reader, I shall recite the actions of the *French* and ourselves together, as a more clear and succinct manner of making those unacquainted with the art of war, more sensible of this important affair.[82]

Colonel *Mercer*, who was then commanding officer of the garrison at *Oswego*, having on the sixth of *August*, intelligence of a large encampment of *French* and *Indians*, about twelve miles off, dispatched one of the schooners, with an account of it to captain *Bradley*[83], who was then on a cruize with the large brigantine and two sloops; at the same time, desired him to cruize as far to the eastward as he could, and to endeavour to prevent the approach of the *French* on the lake; but meeting the next day with a small gale of wind, the large brigantine was drove on shore near *Oswego*, in attempting to get into the harbour; of which misfortune, the *Indians* immediately gave M. de *Montcalm*, the *French* general, notice, who took that opportunity of transporting his heavy cannon to about a mile and a half of the fort, which he could not otherwise have done, had not there been some neglect on our side.

For on the 10th, the first division of the *French* being arrived at *Anse aux Cabannes*, at two o'clock in the morning; the van-guard proceeded at four in the afternoon by land, across woods, to another creek within half a league of *Oswego*, in order to favour the debarkation. At midnight their first division repaired to this creek, and there erected a battery on the lake *Ontario*.

Colonel *Mercer*, in the morning of the 10th, on some canoes being seen to the eastward, sent out the small schooner to make discovery of what they were; she was scarce half a mile from the fort, before she discovered a very large encampment, close under the opposite point, being the first division of the *French* troops abovementioned. On this, the two sloops (the large brigantine being still on shore) were sent out with orders, if possible, to annoy the enemy; but this was to no purpose; the enemy's cannon being large and well pointed, hulled the vessels almost every shot, while theirs fell short of the shore.

This day and the next, the enemy were employed in making gabions, faucissons, and fascines, and in cutting a road cross the woods, from the place of landing, to the place where the trenches were to be opened; and, the second divisions of the enemy arriving on the 11th, in the morning, with the artillery and provisions, the same immediately landed without any opposition. Tho' dispositions were made for opening the trenches on the 10th at night, it was midnight before they could begin the trench, which was rather a parallel of about 100 *Toises*¶ in front, and opened at the distance of 90 Toises from the foss of fort *Ontario*, in ground embarrassed with trunks of trees.

About five in the morning of the 11th, this parallel was finished, and the workmen began to erect the batteries. Thus was the place invested by about 5000 men, and thirty-two pieces of cannon, from twelve to eighteen pounders, besides several large brass mortars and hoyets, (among

---

¶ A *Toise* is a *French* measure, and contains about two fathom or six feet in length.

which artillery was part of general *Braddock*'s.) About noon they began the attack of fort *Ontario*, with small arms, which was briskly returned. All this day the garrison was employed on the West side of the river, in repairing the batteries on the south side of the *Old Fort*.

The next morning, (the 12th), at day-break, a large number of *French* batteaux were discovered on the lake, in their way to join the enemy's camp; on which, colonel *Mercer* ordered the two sloops to be again sent out, with directions to get between the batteaux and the camp; but before our vessels came up, the batteaux had secured themselves under the fire of their cannon.

In the evening, a detachment was made of 100 men of the 50th (general *Pepperell*'s) regiment, and 126 of the *New-Jersey* provincials, under the command of colonel *Schuyler*, to take possession of the fort on the hill, to the Westward of the *Old Fort*, and under the direction of the engineer, Mr. *McKeller*[84], were to put it into the best state of defence they could; in which work, they were employed all the following night.

The enemy on the East-side continued their approaches to the fort *Ontario*, but with their utmost efforts for a long time they could not bring their cannon to bear on it. However, drawing their cannon with great expedition, next morning (the 13th) about ten o'clock, to a battery erected within sixty yards from it; they played them very hotly on the garrison, notwithstanding the constant fire kept on them, and the loss of their principal engineer, who was killed in the trenches. A council of war was immediately held by the officers of general *Pepperell*'s regiment, who observing the mortars were beginning to play, concluded it most advisable to quit fort *Ontario*, and join colonel *Schuyler*'s regiment at fort *George* or fort *Rascal*; and an account of this latter battery being sent to colonel *Mercer*, by the commandant of the enemy, ordering him to evacuate the fort, they accordingly did, about three in the afternoon, destroying the cannon, ammunition, and provisions therein, and managed their retreat so as to pass the river, and join the troops at the West-side without the loss of a man. These troops being about 370, were immediately ordered to join colonel *Schuyler*, which they accordingly did, and were employed all the following night in compleating the works of that fort.

M. *Montcalm* immediately took possession of fort *Ontario*, and ordered the communication of the parallel to be continued to the banks of the river, where, in the beginning of the night, they began a grand battery, placed in such a manner, that it could not only batter fort *Oswego*, and the way from thence to fort *George*, but also the intrenchment of *Oswego*.

In the morning of the 13th, the large brigantine being off the rocks and repaired, a detachment of eighty men of the garrison was put on board of her and the two sloops, in order to go out immediately; but the wind continuing to blow directly into the harbour, rendered it impossible for them to get out before the place was surrendered. This night, as well as the night before, parties of the enemy's irregulars made several attempts to surprize our advance guards and centinels, on the West-side of the river, but did not succeed in any of them.

The enemy were employed this night in bringing up their cannon, and raising a battery. On our side, we kept a constant fire of cannon and shells from the *Old Fort*, and works about it. The cannon which most annoyed the enemy, were four pieces, which we reversed on the platform of an earthen work, which surrounded the *Old Fort*, and which was intirely enfiladed by the enemy's battery on the opposite shore: In this situation, without the least cover, the train, assisted by a detachment of *Shirley*'s regiment, behaved remarkably well.

At day-break on the 14th, we renewed our fire on that part of the opposite shore, where we had the evening before, observed the enemy at work, in raising the battery.

The enemy in three columns, consisting of 2500 *Canadians* and savages, crossed the river, some by swimming, and others by wading, with the water up to their middles, in order to invest and attack the old fort. This bold action, by which they intirely cut off the communication of the two forts; the celerity with which the works were carried on, in ground that we thought impracticable; a continual return of our fire from a battery of ten cannon, twelve pounders; and their preparing a battery of mortars and hoyets, made colonel *Mercer* think it advisable (he not knowing their numbers) to order colonel *Schuyler* with 500 men, to oppose them; which would accordingly have been carried into execution, and consequently, every man of the 500 cut off, had not colonel *Mercer* been killed by a cannon ball, a few minutes after. The resolution of this valiant colonel, seemed to be determined to oppose the *French* to the last extremity, and to maintain his ground at *Oswego*, but his final doom came on so unexpectedly, that his loss was universally regretted.

About ten o'clock, the enemy's battery was ready to play; at which time, all our places of defence, were either enfiladed, or ruined by the constant fire of their cannon; fort *Rascal* or *George*, in particular, having at that time no guns, and scarce in a condition to defend itself against small arms; with 2500 irregulars on our backs, ready to storm us on that side, and 2000 of their regulars as ready to land in our front, under the fire of their cannon. Whereas,

Fort *Rascal* might have been made a very defensible fortress, lying on a hill, and the ascent to it so steep, that had an enemy been ever so numerous, they must have suffered greatly in an attempt to storm it. Why it was not in a better state, it becomes not me to say, but matters were so.

And in this situation we were, when colonel *Littlehales*[85], who succeeded colonel *Mercer* in the command, called a council of war, who were, with the engineers, unanimously of opinion, that the works were no longer tenable; and that it was by no means prudent to risk a storm with such unequal numbers.

The chamade was accordingly ordered to be beat, and the firing ceased on both sides; yet the *French* were not idle, but improved this opportunity to bring up more cannon, and advance the main body of their troops within musquet-shot of the garrison, and prepared every thing for a storm. Two officers were sent to the *French* general, to know what terms he would give; the marquis de *Montcalm* made answer, that they might expect whatever terms were consistent with the service of his *Most Christian* majesty: He accordingly agreed to the following, ---

Article I. "The garrison shall surrender prisoners of war, and shall be conducted from hence to *Montreal*, where they shall be treated with humanity, and every one shall have treatment agreeable to their respective ranks, according to the custom of war.
II. "Officers, and soldiers, and individuals shall have their baggage and cloaths, and they shall be allowed to carry them along with them.
III. "They shall remain prisoners of war, until they are exchanged."
Given at the camp before *Oswego*,
    August 14, 1756
        MONTCALM.

By virtue of this capitulation, the garrison surrendered prisoners of war, and the *French* immediately took possession of *Oswego*, and fort *George*, which they intirely destroyed, agreeable to their orders, after removing the artillery, war-like stores and provisions.

But, to describe the plunder, havock, and devastation, made by the *French*, as well as the savages, who rushed in by thousands, is impossible. For notwithstanding the *Christian* promise made by the general of his *Most Christian* majesty, they all behav'd more like infernal beings than creatures in human shapes. In short, not contented with surrendering upon the above terms, they scalped and killed all the sick and wounded in the hospitals; mangling, butchering, cutting, and chopping off their heads, arms, legs, &c. with spades, hatchets, and other such diabolical instruments; treating the whole with the utmost cruelty, notwithstanding the repeated intercessions of the defenceless sick and wounded for mercy; which were indeed piteous enough to have softened any heart possessed of the minutest particle of humanity!

Here I cannot help observing, that notwithstanding what has been said of the behavior of the officers of these (the 50th and 51st) regiments, I must, with the greatest truth, give them the characters of brave, but I wish I could say, experienced men; every one of them that I had an opportunity of observing during the siege, behaving with the utmost courage and intrepidity. Nor in this place, can I omit particularly naming colonel *James Campbell* and captain *Archibald Hamilton*[**] who assisted with the greatest spirit and alacrity the private men at the great guns. But for such an handful of men as our garrisons then consisted of, and the works being of such a weak and defenceless nature, to have made a longer defence, or have caused the enemy to raise the siege, would have been such an instance as *England* for many years hath not experienced; and I am afraid will be many more before it will, for reasons that are too obvious.

The quantity of stores and ammunition we then had in the three forts is almost incredible. But of what avail are powder and ball if walls and ramparts are defenceless, and men insufficient to make use of men? In short, the *French* by taking this place, made themselves masters of the following things, all which were immediately sent to *Frontenac*, viz. Seven pieces of brass cannon, nineteen, fourteen, and twelve pounders; forty eight iron cannon of nine, six, five, three, and two pounders; a brass mortar of nine inches, four twelfths, and thirteen others of six and three inches; forty seven swivel guns; 23,000 lb. of gun powder; 8000 lb. of lead and musket ball; two thousand nine hundred and fifty cannon balls; one hundred and fifty bombs, of nine inches, and three hundred more, of six inches diameter; one thousand four hundred and seventy six grenadoes; one thousand and seventy musquets; a vessel pierced for eighteen guns; the brigantine of sixteen, a goeletta of ten, a batteaux of ten, (the sloops already mentioned) another of eight guns, a skirff of eighteen swivels, and another burnt upon the stocks; seven hundred and four barrels of biscuit, one thousand three hundred and eighty six firkins of bacon and beef; seven hundred and twelve firkins of meal; thirty two live oxen; fifteen hogs, and a large sum of money in the military chest,

---

[**] Colonel Campbell and Captain Hamilton are at present in Scotland, the former resides near Glasgow, and the latter in Edinburgh.

amounting, as the *French* said, to eighteen thousand five hundred and ninety four livres.

On the 16th they began to remove us; the officers were first sent in batteaux, and two hundred soldiers a day afterwards, till the whole were gone, being carried first to *Montreal*, and from thence to *Quebec*. Our duty in the batteaux till we reached the first place, was very hard and slavish: And during the time we were on the lake or river St. *Laurence*, it appeared very easy and feasible for commodore *Bradely*, had he thought proper, to have destroyed all the enemy's batteaux, and have prevented them from ever landing their cannon within forty miles of the fort. But he knew his own reasons for omitting this piece of service best.

Our party arriving at *Montreal* in *Canada* on the 28th; we were that night secured in the fort, as were the rest as they came in. The *French* used various means to win some of our troops over to their interest, or at least to do their work in the fields, which many refused among whom was myself; who were then conducted on board a ship, and sent to *Quebec* where, on arriving the 5th of *September*, we were lodged in a gaol, and kept for the space of one month.

During this our captivity, many of our men, rather than lie in a prison went out to work, and assist the *French* in getting in their harvest; they having then scarce any people left in that country but old men, women, and children, so that the corn was continually falling into the stubble, for want of hands to reap it: But those who did go out, in two or three days, chose confinement again, rather than liberty on such terms, being almost starved, having nothing in the country to live on but dry bread, whereas we in the prison were each of us allowed two pounds of bread, and half a pound of meat a day, and otherwise treated with a good deal of humanity.

Eighteen soldiers were all the guard they had to place over us, who being greatly fatigued with hard duty, and dreading our rising on them, (which had we had any arms we might easily have done, and ravaged the country round, as it was then intirely defenceless) and the town's people themselves fearing the consequences of having such a number of men in a place where provisions were at that time very scarce and dear, they thought of sending us away, the most eligible way of keeping themselves from famine, and accordingly put 500 of us on board a vessel for *England*.

But before I continue the account of our voyage home to our native country, I shall just make a short retrospection on the consequences which attended the loss of *Oswego*, as appeared to us and the rest of the people at *Quebec*, who knew that part of *America*, to which this important place was a safeguard.

As soon as *Oswego* was taken, our only communication from the *Mohawk*'s river to the lake *Oneida*, was stopt up, by filling the place at *Wood's Creek* with great logs and trees for many miles together. A few days afterwards the forts at the *Great Carrying Place*, and then our most advanced post into the country of the *Six Nations*, which I have before given a short account of, (and where there were at that time above three thousand men, including one thousand two hundred batteaux men, and which still gave the *Six Nations* some hopes that we would defend their country against the *French*) were abandoned and destroyed, and the troops which were under the command of general Webb[86], retreated to *Burnet*'s field[87], and left the country and the *Six Nations* to the mercy of the enemy.

The *French*, immediately after the taking of *Oswego*, demolished, as is said before, all the works there, and returned with their prisoners and booty to *Ticonderoga*[88], to oppose our provincial army under the command of General Winslow, who had shamefully been kept in expectation of the dilatory arrival of Lord *Lowdon* [Loudoun] from attacking *Crown Point*, while the enemy were weak, and it was easily in our power to have beat them.

The consequences of the destruction of our forts at the *Great Carrying Place*, and General *Webb*'s retreating to *Burnet*'s field, is now, alas! too apparent to every one acquainted with *American* affairs. The *Indians* of the *Six Nations* undoubtedly looked upon it as abandoning them and their country to the *French*: for they plainly saw that we had no strong hold near them, and that (by the place at *Wood's Creek* being stopped) we could not if we would afford them any assistance at *Onondago, Cayuga*, and in the *Senekea*'s country, which were their chief castles: That the forts begun by us in those countries were left unfinished, and therefore could be of no use to them, and which, if we had kept the *Carrying Place*, we might have finished, and given them still hopes of our being able to defend.

But despairing of our being further serviceable to them, those *Iroquois*, who were before our friends, and some of the others, have indeed deserted us, and the consequences of such their junctions with the *French* was soon after felt in the loss of *Fort George* on lake *Sacrament*.[89]

The fine country on the *Mohawk*'s river down to *Albany*, was by this step left open to the ravages of the enemy, and an easy passage opened to the *French* and their *Indians* into the provinces of *Pensylvania* and

New Jersey, by the way of *Susquehanna* and *Delaware* rivers, which were before covered by our settlements on the *Mohawks* river, and the *Six Nations*.

I shall here give the best description of the *Indians*, their way of living, &c. in my power.

It is difficult to guess what may be the number of the *Indians* scattered up and down our back settlements; but, if their own account be true, they amount to many thousands. Be this, however, as it will, they are not to be feared merely on account of their numbers; other circumstances conspire to make them formidable: The *English* inhabitants, though numerous, are extended over a vast track of land, 500 leagues in length on the sea-shore, and for the most part have fixed habitations, the easiest and shortest passages to which, the *Indians*, by constantly hunting in the woods, are perfectly well acquainted with; and as their way of making war is by sudden attacks upon exposed places, as soon as they have done the mischief at one place, they retire, and either go home by some different route, or go to some distant place to renew their attacks. If they are pursued, it is a chance if they do not ensnare their pursuers; or if that be not the case, as soon as they have gained the rivers, so dexterous are they in the use of their canoes, that they presently get out of reach. It is to no purpose to follow them to their settlements; for they can, without much disadvantage, quit their old habitations, and betake themselves to new ones: Add to this, that they can be suddenly drawn together from any distance, as they can find their subsistence in travelling from their guns.

No people on earth have a higher sense of liberty, or stronger affection for their relations; when offended, they are the most implacable vindictive enemies on earth; for no distance of place, or space of time will abate their resentment; but they will watch every opportunity of revenge, and when such opportunity offers, they revenge themselves effectually.

They will sooner sacrifice their own lives for the sake of liberty, than humble themselves to the arbitrary controul of any person whatsoever. In battle they never submit, and will die rather than be taken prisoners.

Our late transactions in *America* testify, that the friendship of the *Indians* is to be desired, and the only way to maintain a friendly correspondence with them, is by making such propositions to them as will secure their liberties, and be agreeable to their expectations; and not only by keeping these propositions inviolable as well in time of peace as in time of war, but also renewing our treaties with them from time to time; for they are very jealous and tenacious of an affront or neglect. They are very proud, and love to be esteemed. In time of peace, they live upon what they get of the white people, for which they barter skins, furs, &c. Their cloathing, and every thing else they want, such as arms, they get in the same manner. In war-time, they live upon what they can procure by their gun, and if that fails, upon roots, fruits, herbs, and other vegetables of the natural produce of the earth.

They have never the foresight to provide necessaries for themselves; they look only to the present moment, and leave to-morrow to provide for itself. They eat of every wild beast, which they kill without distinction. They always prefer game to vegetables; but when they cannot get venison, they live on roots, fruits and herbs. They destroy a great deal of meat at a time when they have it in their power, and when they leave any, be it never such a great quantity, it is ten to one if any of them will take the trouble to carry a pound of it, but will rather leave it behind them; yet notwithstanding this extravagance, such is their tempers, and they are so inured to hardships, that if they cannot conveniently get at food, they can, and actually do fast sometimes for near a week together, and yet are as active as if they lived regularly. All their spare time is taken up in contriving schemes to succeed in their intended expeditions. They can never be taken in a pursuit by any European. They will travel seventy miles a day, and continue for months together, as I have reason to know from experience, and they are sure to bring their Pursuers into a snare if they are not wary, and have some Indians on their side to beat the bushes. When they are overtaken with sleep, they light a great fire, which prevents the wild beasts from falling upon them; for wild beasts have a natural aversion to fire; nor is it easy for an enemy to discover them in this condition; for the country is one continued tract of thick wood, overgrown with brush-wood, so that you cannot see the fire till you be within a few yards of it. They have nothing covering them from the inclemency of the weather but a blanket put upon them, something in the shape of a Highlander's plaid.

And further, to prevent their being long observed by their pursuers, or to be seen too soon when they have a mind to attack any plantation, they paint themselves of the same colour with the trees among which they hide themselves.

When they are to attack a plantation they never come out till night, and then they rush instantly upon the farms, &c. and destroy every thing, as well men, women and children, as beasts; then they fall to plunder, and return to their lurking-holes till another opportunity of plunder happens, when they renew their attack in the same manner; so that if some method is not taken to draw them into our interest, our colonies will be in a continual alarm, and the country will soon become desolate; for no body will venture their lives to settle on the back parts, unless the Indians are our friends.

The Indian manner of fighting is quite different from that of other nations. They industriously avoid all open engagements; and, besides ambuscades, their principal way is bush fighting, in the exercise of which they are very dexterous; for the back-country being one continued wood, except some few spots cleared for the purpose of husbandry by our back settlers, the Indians squat themselves down behind the trees, and fire their muskets at the enemy; if the enemy advances, then they retreat behind other trees, and fire in the same manner; and as they are good marksmen they never fire in vain, whereas their pursuers seldom hit.

Notwithstanding the politic schemes of France are nearly brought to a period, yet if the Indians are not satisfied with the conclusion of a peace betwixt us and the French as to America; I mean, unless they are fairly dealt with, we shall gain but little by all our conquest; for it is the friendship of the Indians that will make Canada valuable to us. We have already more lands than we are able to manage; but the advantage, nay the necessity of keeping Canada I have already shown; and therefore I shall go on with my account of the Indians.

When last in London, I remember to have heard some coffeehouse politicians, chagrined at the devastation they made on our back settlements, say, that it would be an easy matter to root out the savages by clearing the ground. I answer, that the task may seem easy to them, but the execution of such a scheme on such a tract of land, would be so difficult that I doubt whether there are people enough in Great Britain and Ireland to accomplish it in a hundred years time, were they to meet with no opposition; but where there is such a subtle enemy to deal with, I am afraid we should make but little progress in reducing the Indians, even allowing the country to be all cleared, there are hills and other fortresses to which the Indians can retire, and where they would greatly have the better of every attempt to dislodge them. The only way I would advise is to keep friends with the Indians, and endeavour to prevail on them to settle in the same manner as the Planters do, which they will be the more easily brought to, if the French are excluded from Canada. For notwithstanding their wandring way of life, I have the greatest reason to believe they have no dislike to an easy life. And as they will have no temptations to murder, as they had when stirred up by the subjects of his most Christian Majesty, they will soon become useful members of society.

When first the *English* arrived in the *American* colonies, they found the woods inhabited by a race of people, uncultivated in their manners, but not quite devoid of humanity. They were strangers to literature, ignorant of the liberal arts, and destitute of almost every conveniency of life.

But if they were unpracticed in the arts of more civilized nations, they were also free from their vices. They seemed perfect in two parts of the ancient Persian education, namely, in shooting with the bow, and speaking truth. In their dealings they commonly exchange one commodity for another. Strangers themselves to fraud, they had an entire confidence in others. According to their abilities, they were generous and hospitable. Happy, thrice happy had they been, if, still preserving their native innocence and simplicity, they had only been instructed in the knowledge of God, and the doctrines of Christianity. Had they been taught some of the more useful parts of life, and to lay aside what was wild and savage in their manners!

They received the *English*, upon their first arrival, with open arms, treated them kindly, and shewed an earnest desire, that they should settle and live with them. They freely parted with some of their lands to their new come brethren, and chearfully entered into a league of friendship with them. As the *English* were in immediate want of the assistance of the *Indian*, they, on their part, endeavoured to make their coming agreeable. Thus they lived for some years, in the mutual exchange of friendly offices. Their houses were open to each other: they treated one another as brothers. But by their different way of living, the *English* soon acquired property, while the Indians continued in their former indigence; hence the former found they could easily live without the latter, and therefore became less anxious about preserving their friendship. This gave a check to that mutual hospitality that had hitherto subsisted between them; and this, together with the decrease of game for hunting, arising from the increase of the English settlements, induced the *Indians* to remove further back into the woods.

From this time the natives began to be treated as a people of whom an advantage might be taken. As the trade with them was free and open, men of loose and abandoned characters engaged in it, and practiced every fraud. Before the coming of the white people, the Indians never tasted spirituous liquors, and like most barbarous nations, having once tasted, became immoderately fond thereof, and had no longer any government of themselves. The traders availed themselves of this weakness; instead of carrying our cloaths to cover the naked savages, they carried them rum, and thereby debauched their manners, weakened their constitutions, introduced disorders unknown to them before, and in short corrupted and ruined them.

The Indians finding the ill effects of this trade, began to complain. Wherefore laws were made, prohibiting any from going to trade with them without a licence from the Governor, and it was also made lawful for the Indians to stave the casks, and spill what rum was brought among them: but this was to little purpose: the Indians had too little command of themselves to do their duty, and were easily prevailed upon not to execute this law; and the design of the former was totally evaded, by men of some character taking out licences to trade, and then employing under them persons of no honour or principle, generally servants and convicts transported hither from Britain and Ireland, whom they sent with goods into the Indian country to trade on their account. These getting beyond the reach of the law, executed unheard of villanies upon the poor natives, committing crimes which modestly forbids to name, and behaving in a manner too shocking to be related.

At every treaty which the Indians held with the English, they complained of the abuses they suffered from the traders, and trade as then carried on. They requested that the traders might be recalled; but all to no purpose. They begged in the strongest terms, that no rum might be suffered to come among them; but were only told that they were at liberty to spill all the rum brought into their country. At this time, little or no pains were taken to civilize or instruct them in the Christian religion, till at length the conduct of the traders, professing themselves of that religion, gave the Indians an almost invincible prejudice against it. Besides, as these traders travelled among distant nations of the Indians, and were in some sort the representatives of the English, from them the Indians formed a very unfavourable opinion of our whole nation, and easily believed every misrepresentation made of us by our enemies. There are instances in history, where the virtue and disinterested behaviour of one man, have prejudiced whole nations of barbarians in favour of the people to whom he belonged; and it is then to be wondered at, if the Indians conceived a rooted prejudice against us, when not one, but a whole set of men, namely, all of our nation that they had an opportunity of seeing or conversing with, were persons of a loose or abandoned behaviour, insincere and faithless, without religion, virtue, or morality. No one will think I exaggerate these matters, who has either known the traders themselves, or who has read the public treaties.

If to this be added, what I find in the late treaties, that they have been wronged in some of their lands, what room will there be any longer to wonder that we have so little interest with them, that their conduct towards us is of late so much changed, that, instead of being a security and protection to us, as they have been hitherto, during the several wars between us and the French, they are now turned against us and become our enemies, principally on account of the fraudulent dealings and immoral conduct of those heretofore employed in our trade with them, who have brought dishonor upon our religion and disgrace on our nation? It nearly concerns us, if possible, to wipe off these reproaches, and to redeem our character, which can only be done by regulating the trade. And this the Indians, with whom the government of Philadelphia lately treated, demanded and expected of us.

At present a favourable opportunity presents for doing it effectually. All those who were engaged in this trade, are by the present troubles removed from it, and it is to be hoped that the legislature will fall upon measures to prevent any such from ever being concerned in it again. This is the only foundation upon which we can expect a lasting peace with the natives. It is evident, that a great deal depends upon the persons who are to be sent into the Indian country: from these alone the Indians will form a judgment of us, our religion and manners. If these then who are to be our representatives among the Indians, be men of virtue and integrity, sober in their conversation, honest in their dealings, and whose practice corresponds with their profession, the judgment formed of us will be favourable: if, on the contrary, they be loose and profane persons, men of wicked lives, and profligate morals, we must expect that among the Indians, our religion will pass for a jest, and we in general for a people faithless and despicable.

I might here add some observations respecting the commodities proper to be carried among the Indians, in kind as well as quality, with a method of carrying on the trade, so as to preserve the native innocence of the Indians, and at the same time confirm them immoveable in our interest; but these things, as well as some remarks I have in a course of years made upon the Indians, I shall leave for the subject of some future history.

I shall now proceed to give a concise account of the climates, produce, trade, &c. of North America. And first,

Of NEW - ENGLAND.

The province of New England appears to be vastly extensive, being about 400 miles in length, and near 300 in breadth, situated between 69 and 73 deg. W. Long. and between 41 and 46 deg. N. Lat. It was first settled by the Independents, a little before the commencement of the civil wars in England: They transported themselves thither, rather than they would communicate with the church of England.

The lands next the sea in New-England, are generally low, and the soil sandy; but farther up the country it rises into hills, and on the Northeast it is rocky and mountainous: The winters are much severer here than in Old England, though it lies 9 or 10 degrees more south, but they have usually a clearer sky and more settled weather, both in winter and summer, than in Old England; and though their summers are shorter, the air is considerably hotter while it lasts. The winds are very boisterous in the winter season, and the North wind blowing over a long tract of frozen and uncultivated countries, with several fresh water lakes, makes it excessive cold. Their rivers are sometimes congealed in a night's time; the climate is generally healthful, and agreeable to English constitutions.

The fruits of Old England come to great perfection here, particularly peaches, which are planted trees; and we have commonly 1200 or 1400 fine peaches on such a tree at one time; nay, of the fruit of one single apple tree in one season, nine barrels of cyder have been made. English wheat I find does not thrive here, within 40 or 50 miles of Boston; but farther up in the country they have it in great plenty, and I think it comes to the same perfection as in Britain. Now, why wheat should not grow near this city I confess I can assign no reason that will fully satisfy the reader's curiosity. The conjectures upon it are various: Some venture to say, that it was occasioned by the unjust persecution of the Quakers, the Independents having vented their spleen against them in a way the most rigorous, and in flat contradiction to the laws of christianity. All other grain but wheat thrives in this place with great success; in particular Indian corn, one grain whereof frequently produces 1200, and sometimes 2000 grains. This corn is of three different colors, viz. blue, white and yellow.

Of NEW - YORK.

The situation of this province is between 72 and 76 West long. and between 41 and 44 North lat. being about 200 miles in length, and 100 miles in breadth. The lands, in the Jerseys and South part of New-York, are low and flat; but as you ascend 20 or 30 miles up Hudson's river, the country is rocky and mountainous. The air is much milder here in winter than in New-England, and in summer it is pretty much the same. The produce and trade of New-York and the Jerseys consist in cattle and a good breed of horses. They have plenty of wheat and other grain, such as Indian corn, buck-weed, oats, barley, and rye. It abounds also with store of fish; they supply the sugar islands with flour, salt-beef, pork, salt-fish, and the timber-planks, in return for the produce raised there.

Of PENSYLVANIA.

The extent of this colony is 200 miles in length, and 200 miles in breadth. The soil is much better than in Jersey, chiefly consisting of a black mold; the country rises gradually as in the adjacent provinces, having the Apalachian mountains on the West, and is divided into six counties. The air, it lying in the 40 deg. of N. lat. is near the same as in New-York, and very healthy to English constitutions. The produce and merchandize of Pensylvania consists in horses, pipe staves, beef, pork, salt fish, skins, furrs, and all sorts of grain, viz. wheat, rye, pease, oats, barley, buck-weed, Indian corn, Indian pease, beans, pot-ashes, wax, &c. and in return for these commodities, they import from the Carribee islands, and other places, rum, sugar, molasses, silver, negroes, salt, and wine; and from Great Britain, houshold goods, cloathing of all sorts, hardware, &c. The nature of the soil in Pensylvania, the Jerseys, and New-York, is extremely proper to produce hemp, flax, &c.

If the government of Pensylvania, since the death of its first proprietor William Penn, had taken proper methods to oblige the traders to deal justly with the Indians, whose tempers, when exasperated with resentment, are more savage than the hungry lion; these disasters might have been, in good degree, prevented.

I intend to conclude this argument in a few words and shall endeavour to do justice on both sides, by adhering strictly to truth. Know, therefore, that within these late years the Indians being tolerably acquainted with the nature of our commerce, have detected the roguery of some of the traders, whereupon they lodged many and grievous complaints to Col. Weiser, the interpreter between them and the English, of the injurious and fraudulent usage they had received for several years backwards from white people, who had cheated them out of their skins and furrs, not giving them one quarter their value for them.

Likewise they remonstrated, that whereas hunting was the chief way or art they ever had to earn a livelihood by; game was now become very scarce, because the whites practiced it so much on their ground, destroying their prey. Colonel Weiser, their interpreter, advised them to bring down their skins and furrs to Philadelphia themselves, promising that he would take proper care to see their goods vended to their advantage. Whereupon they did so, in pursuance of his instructions, and finding it their interest, resolved to continue in the way he had chalked out for them; for now they were supplied with every thing they wanted from the merchants shops, at the cheapest rates. And thus it plainly appeared to the Indians, that they had been long imposed on by the traders, and therefore they were determined to have no more dealings with them. This conduct and shyness of the Indians was very disagreeable to several gentlemen of the province, who were nearly interested in that species of commerce.

Accordingly, in the years 1753 and 1754, some of the traders had the assurance to renew their friendship with them, when, instead of remitting them clothes and other necessaries as had been usual, and were most proper for them, they, with insidious purposes, carried them large quantities of rum in small casks, which they knew the natives were fond of, under colour of giving it them *gratis*. In this manner were the savages inveigled into liquor by the whites, who took the opportunity while they were intoxicated of going off with their skins and furrs; but the natives, recovering from the debauch, soon detected the villainy, and, in revenge, killed many of the traders, and went directly over to the French, who encouraged them to slay every English person they could meet with, and destroy their houses by fire, giving them orders to spare neither man, woman, nor child. Besides, as a farther incitement to diligence in this bloody task, they promised the savages the reward of 15 *l.* sterling, for every scalp they should take, on producing the same before any of his *most christian* Majesty's officers; civil or military.

Thus our perfidious enemies instigated those unreasonable barbarians to commence acts of depredation, violence and murder on the several inhabitants in North America in 1754, and more especially in Pensylvania, as knowing it to be the most defenceless province on the continent. This consideration prompted the savage race to exhaust their malicious fury on it in particular.

Of MARYLAND.

This country extends about 150 miles in length, and 137 miles in breadth. The lands are low and flat next the sea; towards the heads of rivers they rise into hills, and beyond lie the Apalachian Mountains, which are exceeding high. The air of this province is excessive hot some part of the summer, and equally cold in the winter, when the North-west wind blows; but the winters are not of so long duration here as in some other colonies adjoining to it. In the spring of the year they are infested with thick heavy fogs that rise from the low lands, which render the air more unhealthy for English constitutions; and hence it is, that in the aforesaid season the people are constantly afflicted with agues.

The produce of this country is chiefly tobacco, planted and cultivated here with much application, and nearly the same success as in Virginia, and their principal trade with England is in that article. It also affords them most sorts of the grain and fruits of Europe and America.

Of VIRGINIA.

The extent of this province is computed to be 260 miles in length, and 220 miles in breadth, being mostly low, flat land. For one hundred miles up the country, there is scarce a hill or a stone to be seen. The air and seasons (it lying between 36 and 39 of North Lat.) depend very much on the wind as to heat and cold, dryness and moisture. The North and Northwest winds are very nitrous and piercing cold, or else boisterous and stormy: The South and South-east winds, hasy and sultry hot. In winter they have a fine clear air, which renders it very pleasant: The frosts are short, but sometimes so very sharp that rivers are froze over three miles broad. Snow often falls in large quantities; but seldom continues above two or three days at most.

The soil, though generally sandy and shallow, produces tobacco of the best quality in great abundance. The people's usual food is Indian corn made into hommony, boiled to a pulp, and comes the nearest to buttered wheat of any thing I can compare it to. They have horses, cows, sheep, and hogs in prodigious plenty; many of the last running wild in the woods. The regulation kept here is much the same as in New-England; every man from 16 to 60 years of age is inlisted into the militia, and mustered once a year, at a general review, and four times a year by troops and companies. Their military complement, by computation, amounts to about 30,000 effective men, the collective number of the inhabitants, men, women and children, to 100,500 and including servants and slaves, to twice that number.

Of CAROLINA.

This colony is computed to extend 660 miles in length; but its breadth is unknown. The lands here are generally low and flat, and not a hill to be seen from St. Augustine to Virginia, and a great way beyond. 'Tis mostly covered with woods where the planters have not cleared it. About 100 miles west of the coast, it shoots up into eminences, and continues to rise gradually all along to the Apalachian Mountains, which are about 160 miles distant from the ocean. The North parts of Carolina are very uneven, but the ground is extremely proper for producing wheat; and all other sorts of grain that grow in Europe will come to great perfection here. The South parts of Carolina, if properly cultivated, might be made to produce silk, wine, and oil. This country yields large quantities of rice, of which they yearly ship off to other colonies about 80,000 barrels, each barrel containing 400 weight, besides they make abundance of tar, pitch, and turpentine. They carry on also a great trade with deer-skins, and furrs, to all places of Europe, which the English receive from the Indians in barter for guns, powder, knives, scissors, looking-glasses, beads, rum, tobacco, coarse-cloath, &c.

The English chapmen carry these pack-horses 5 or 600 miles into the country, West of Charles-Town; but most of the commerce is confined within the limits of the Creek and Cherokee nations, which do not lie above 350 miles from the coast. The air is very temperate and agreeable both summer and winter. Carolina is divided into two distinct provinces, viz. North and South Carolina.

Of NOVA - SCOTIA.

This place extends about 600 miles in length, and 450 in breadth: The air is pretty much the same as in Old England: The soil is, for the most part, barren; but where it is cleared and cultivated, it affords good corn and pasture. Here is fine timber, and fit for building, from whence pitch and tar may be extracted. Here also hemp and flax will grow, so that this country will be capable of furnishing all manner of naval stores. It abounds likewise with deer, wild fowl, and all sorts of game. On the coast is one of the finest cod-fisheries in the world. European cattle, viz. sheep, oxen, swine, horses, &c. they have in great abundance. The winters are very cold, their frosts being sharp and of a long duration: Their summers are moderately hot, so that the climate, in the main, seems to be agreeable to English constitutions.

Of CANADA.

I shall close the description of the American colonies, with a short account of the soil and produce of French Canada. Its extent is, according to their map, 1800 miles in length, and 1260 in breadth. The soil, in the low lands near the river St. Laurence, will, indeed, raise wheat; but, withal, I found it so shallow, that it would not produce that grain above two years, unless it was properly manured. About 20 miles from the said river, so hilly and mountainous is the country, that nothing but Indians and wild ravenous beasts resort there. However, they have plenty of rye, Indian corn, buck-weed, and oats; likewise of horses, cows, sheep, swine, &c. But I have observed that fruits of any kind do not come to such perfection here, as in some of the English settlements, which is owing to the long duration and excessive cold of their winters. The summer is short and temperately hot. The climate, in general, is healthy and agreeable to European constitutions. And so much for the provinces in North-America.

It is now high time to return to the embarkation at Quebec. Five hundred of us, being to be sent to England, were put on board La Renomme, a French paquet-boat, Captain Dennis Vitree commander: we sailed under a flag of truce, and though the French behaved with a good deal of politeness, yet we were almost starved for want of provisions. One biscuit, and two ounces of pork a day, being all our allowance, and half dead with cold, having but few clothes, and the vessel being so small, that the major part of us were obliged to be upon deck in all weathers. After a passage of six weeks, we at last, to our great joy, arrived at Plymouth on the sixth of November 1756. But there our troubles and hardships were not, as we expected, put to a period for some time; scruples arising to the commissaries and admiral there, about taking us on shore, as there was no cartel agreed on between the French and English, we were confined on board, until the determination of the Lords of the Admiralty should be known; lying there in a miserable condition seven or eight days, before we received orders to disembark, which, when we were *permitted* to do, being ordered from thence, in different parties to Totnes, Kingsbridge, Newtown-Bushel, Newtown-Abbot in Devonshire, I was happy in being quartered at Kingsbridge, where I met with such civility and entertainment, as I had for a long time been a stranger to.

In about four months we were again ordered to Plymouth-Dock, to be draughted into other regiments; where, on being inspected, I was, on account of the wound I had received in my hand, discharged as *incapable* of *further* service; and was allowed the sum of six Shillings to carry me home to Aberdeen, near the place of my nativity.[90] But finding that sum insufficient to subsist me half the way, I was obliged to make my application to the honourable gentlemen of the city of York, where, on considering my necessity and reviewing my manuscript on the transactions of the Indians, herein before-mentioned, thought proper to have it printed for my own benefit, which they cheerfully subscribed unto. And after disposing of several of my books through the shire, I took the first opportunity of going in quest of my relations at Aberdeen, where I received very barbarous usage and ill treatment, occasioned by complaining against the illegal practice of *kidnapping*, in the beginning of my book, which I shall hereafter finally describe in the following pages.

A DISCOURSE on KIDNAPPING.[91]

With proper directions for tradesmen, and others, to avoid slavery, when transported from their native country, by the instigation of perfidious traders.

TO make the subject of the ensuing pages the more accurate and distinct, I shall, in the *first* place, begin with the proceedings of the Magistrates of Aberdeen, when I arrived in that town in June 1758, after having completed the period of my slavery, as related in the beginning of this narrative. No sooner had I offered this little work to sale in that town, which was then my only mean of subsistence, than I was arraigned in a summary complaint at the instance of the magistrates, before their own tribunal, and carried by three or four town-officers to the bar of that tremendous court of Judicature. The complaint exhibited against me contained in substance, "That I had been guilty of causing print, and of publishing and dispersing, this scurrilous and infamous libel, reflecting greatly upon the characters and reputations of the merchants in Aberdeen, and on the town in general, without any ground or reason; whereby the corporation of the city and whole members thereof were greatly hurt and prejudged; and that therefore I ought to be exemplarly punished in my person and goods; and that the said pamphlet, and whole copies thereof, ought to be seized and publicly burnt." Such was the tenor of the complaint; and instead of allowing me an opportunity of taking advice, in time to prepare for my defence, I was hurried before them, and concussed by threats of imprisonment to make a declaration of a very extraordinary cast, and dictated by themselves; bearing, that "I had no ground for advancing and uttering the calumnies, mentioned in my book, against the merchants in Aberdeen, *but the fancy I took in my younger years, which stuck on my memory, tho' I did not find that I had reason so to do; nor did I believe these things to be true;* and that I was willing to contradict in a public manner what I had so advanced, &c."

After eliciting this declaration, the magistrates, without adjournment, "appointed me to find caution to stand trial on the said complaint at any time when called for, and imprisoned till performance; and ordered all the copies of my pamphlet to be lodged in the clerks chamber." My books were accordingly seized, and myself committed to the custody of the town-officers, who conducted me to jail, and where I must have lain till next day, had not my landlord bailed me out. Next forenoon the magistrates proceeded to sentence on their own complaint; and accordingly they "ordained the offensive leaves of all the copies of the said pamphlet to be cut out, and publicly burnt at the market-cross by the hands of the common hangman, the town officers attending and publishing the cause of the burning; that I should give in a signed declaration of much the same tenor with the former; begging pardon of the magistrates and merchants in the most-submissive manner, and desiring this my recantation to be inserted in the York news-papers, or any other news-papers they should think proper; and also ordained me to be incarcerated in the tolbooth, till I granted the said declaration; and ammerciated[92] me in ten shillings sterling, under the pain of imprisonment; and immediately after to remove out of town."

Such was the sentence of the magistrates of Aberdeen against me, every particular of which was forthwith put in execution in the most rigorous manner. Had these judges had the least reflection, they must have been conscious, that, in every step of their procedure, they were committing the grossest abuse. The complaint was made by their order and direction, and served at their own instigation, by which means they were first the Accusers, and afterwards the Condemners. The subject of it was so irrelevant, that they must have been sensible they were prosecuting an innocent man, for relating the melancholy particulars of his life, which ought to have rendered him rather an object of their protection, than of their malice. The facts he had set forth in his pamphlet, relating to the original of his misfortunes, were so flagrant, that, had he sued for it, he was intitled to redress against the authors of his miseries, from those very magistrates who now had the cruelty to aggravate them, by inflicting additional hardships. To pretend ignorance is a very lame excuse. He must have been a very youthful magistrate in 1758, who could not remember some circumstances of a public branch of trade carried on in 1744. It is inconceivable, that, of a whole bench of magistrates, no less than six in number, not one was of an age capable of recollecting what had happened only fourteen years before; nor is it to be presumed, that, of almost all the inhabitants of Aberdeen, they alone, who had the best access to know the traffick of the town, should remain ignorant of a commerce, which was carried on in the market-places, on the high streets, and in the avenues to the town, in the most public manner. Neither of these suppositions will easily gain credit. The magistrates are commonly of such an age, and ought to be men of such reflection, as to render the first impossible; and the second, for the reasons given above, is equally incredible. Every impartial person must therefore be persuaded that the magistrates were not unacquainted with that illicit species of trade openly carried on in that city about the year 1744, and prior to that period. To prove that there was such an infamous traffick, I appeal to the depositions of several witnesses, some of whom shared in the calamity by the loss of their children and other relations. These I have subjoined, as they occur in the proof taken on my part, by way of foot notes to this treatise.††

From these vouchers it appears, that the trade of carrying off boys to the plantations in America, and selling them there as slaves, was carried on at Aberdeen, as far down as the year 1744, with an amazing effrontery. It was not carried on in secret, or by stealth, but publicly, and by open violence. The whole neighbouring country were alarmed at it. They would not allow their children to go to Aberdeen, for fear of being kidnapped. When they kept them at home, emissaries were sent out by the merchants, who took them by violence from their parents, and carried them off. If a child was amissing, it was immediately suspected, that he was kidnapped by the Aberdeen merchants; and upon inquiry that was often found to be the case; and so little pains were taken to conceal them, when in the possession of the merchants, that they were driven in flocks through the town, under the inspection of a keeper, who overawed them with a whip, like so many sheep carrying to the slaughter. Not only were these flocks of unhappy children locked up in barns, and places of private confinement, but even the tolbooth and public workhouses were made receptacles for them, and a town-officer employed in keeping them. Parties of worthless fellows, like press-gangs, were hired to patrole the streets, and seize by force such boys as seemed proper subjects for the slave-trade. The practice was but too general. The names of no less than fifteen merchants concerned in this trade, are mentioned

---

†† In the original, Williamson inserted the excerpts from the depositions as footnotes to this essay, some of which grew quite long and ran over several pages. For ease of reading, I have converted these footnotes to text that has been appended at the end of this essay (pp. 79–96). [Editor]

in the proof: And when so many are singled out by the witnesses, it is hardly to be imagined it should be confined to these only, but that they must have omitted many, who were either principals, or abettors and decoys in this infamous traffic. Some of the witnesses depone, that it was the general opinion, that the Magistrates themselves had a hand in it. But what exceeds every proof, and is equal to an acknowledgment, is, that from a book of accompts, recovered on leading the proof, recording the expences laid out on one cargo of these unfortunate objects, it appears, that no less than sixty-nine boys and girls were carried over to America along with me, all of whom suffered the same fate of being ship-wreck'd, and many of them that of being sold as slaves.

After such a demonstration of my veracity and the mal-treatment I had formerly suffered, the reader, 'tis believed, cannot but reflect with some degree of indignation on the iniquitous sentence of the Magistrates of Aberdeen, and commiserate the dismal situation to which I was reduced in consequence of that tyrannical decision. Stript at once of my all, and of my only mean of subsistence, branded with the character of a vagrant and imposter, and stigmatized as such in the Aberdeen Journal[93], banished from the capital of the country wherein I was born, and left to the mercy of the wide world, loaded with all the infamy that malice could invent. What a deplorable situation this! I could not help considering myself in a more wretched state, to be reduced to submit to such barbarities in a civilized country, and the place of my nativity, than when a captive among the savage Indians, who boast not of humanity.

Conscious of my own integrity, and fired with resentment at the indignities poured upon me by this arbitrary decree, I was, by the advice and assistance of some worthy friends, induced to raise a process of oppression and damages against these my judges, before the court of Session, the supreme tribunal of justice. And as the Lord Ordinary was pleased to allow both parties a proof at large, under the sanction of his authority, I ventured to revisit the city from which I had been formerly banished, where, in spite of all the disadvantages with which power, wealth, and influence could overwhelm me, I was enabled to lead such a proof, as convinced that most honourable and impartial bench to which I now appealed, that I had met with the highest injury and injustice, and induced them to decern a suitable redress. For the satisfaction of the reader the substance of this proof is subjoined, as before mentioned.

The following pages, when duly considered, will be obvious to the meanest capacity, as the subject is intirely calculated to open the eyes of the deluded poor, many of whom have suffered tribulation for the loss of their children, whom the ties of nature bind every christian parent to preserve and cherish as their own lives: For as it is absurd to imagine that any parent, tho' in ever so necessitous a condition, would dispose of their own flesh and blood to strangers, who make a prey of innocent children, to accumulate their ill-gotten wealth and support their grandeur, by conveying the unhappy victims to the remotest parts of the globe, where they can have no redress for the injuries done them, these cautions are offered to prevent their falling into the snare.

Sensible I am that what I have already said against my first prosecutors, quadrates with the truth in every particular, and that many unfortunate persons have been involved in misery, and decoyed into slavery and bondage, as well as myself. Separated from their dearest relations, and obliged tamely to submit to the caprice and chastisement of arbitrary masters, who have less pity and compassion on them than on their very beasts of burden. Hard fate to suffer all this! harder still to be prosecuted for telling the interesting tale! I speak this by woeful experience, as well as from the knowledge of the hard fate of several young people of the neighbourhood of my nativity, whether [whither] I had gone in quest of my relations. After so long an absence, my personal appearance must, no doubt, recall to the memory of my friends the manner of my being carried off in my infancy, and they must receive me with wonder and amazement, whom they had for many years deemed for lost. The satisfaction my presence gave them, of which they had been so long deprived, is not to be expressed, and the comfort I enjoyed in the prospect of seeing my nearest relations, was in some degree a solace for the miseries I had undergone: But, even in this, hard fortune pursued me still, and my troubles were not yet at an end. New enemies started up, who, as if the abettors of those who laid the snare for me when a child, now contrived a new species of captivity for me, when I was a man. They begrudged me my liberty, and the freedom I took to relate my misfortunes; in order, therefore, to suppress a disagreeable truth, they again deprived me of it for a time; destroyed my means of subsistence, and loaded me with infamy and reproach; from which, thanks to the justice of my cause and the integrity of my judges, I have at last been honourably delivered. KIDNAPPING, a species of trade followed by these monsters of impiety for the lust of gain, may be compared to the practice of the savages formerly mentioned, who, to gratify their propensity to mischief, cut, mangle, burn and destroy, all the innocent people they can catch. And surely the guilt of the kiddnapper must be much greater than that of the savage race, who boast not of humanity. If the latter commit such crimes, it is against those they imagine to be their enemies, for the sake of plunder; but the former are void of all excuse. What then can some of the *worthy* merchants of Aberdeen say for themselves. Prompted by avarice, and despising the laws of God and all civilized nations, have they not been guilty of this attrocious crime? And does not the blood of the innocent, several of whom have died under the hands of their cruel masters, cry against them for vengaence? Certain it is, that this execrable practice of kiddnapping was put in execution from the year 1740 and downwards, by several merchants in that city, some of whom, for reasons too well known, have since deserted their country. I remember that, much about that time, there were idle fellows employed by those traders, to cajole and decoy, men, women and children, to serve in the plantations in America. The poor deluded parents, being ignorant of the nature of the traffick, and equally ignorant how or where to apply for redress, were obliged to rely on the fair promises of the merchants, whose delusions proved fatal to many of the unhappy victims who were even come of age, and much more so to infants from six to fourteen years, who were incapable to contract for themselves, and transported without the knowledge or consent of their parents. These were left to lament the loss of their children; many of them without the consolation of knowing what had become of them, and who could only imagine that an untimely end had been their fate. Such, it is to be supposed, were the dreadful apprehensions that filled the eyes of my aged parent with tears, from whom I was thus separated in my non-age. What heart can be unmoved with pity at the relation of so dismal a tale? Who can think, without horror, on these monsters of impiety, who could make a traffick of their fellow creatures in a Christian country, almost as openly as is practiced on the coast of Guinea. *Quis talia fando temperet a lachrimis* [who can relate such woes without a tear]? And here the following queries occur, which will tend to explain the meaning of kidnapping.

I. Whether or not, When children are either carried off by force, or decoyed by fraud, without the consent, or without the knowledge, of their parents, in a state of infancy, or under the years of pupillarity, and incapable of entering into a contract or indenture, may not this be called KIDNAPPING?

II. Whether or not, The shutting these Children up in prisons, or places of confinement, in order to make sure of them as a prey, and conceal them from their parents, is not contrary to law, and an attrocious crime?

III. If these proceedings were agreeable to law, and the inclinations of the persons so imprisoned; what occasion was there for confinement? When a person inlists himself in any service as a volunteer, where is the necessity for putting him in prison? But,

IV. If these proceedings were contrary to all laws, human and divine, What punishment can be inflicted adequate to the crime?

My Betrayers well knew the impracticability of making children abide by any obligation extorted from them, or any agreement to which they were decoyed; and therefore they confined us in barns, on board ships, and other convenient places; and, to make our time pass away the more insensibly and free of reflection, they entertained us with music, cards, and other childish diversions, till such time as they had got their complement, and the ship was ready to sail.

Various were the arts and stratagems made use of to inveigle these unhappy creatures. Some were insnared by receiving a triffle of money, and then told they were fairly inlisted. Others were tempted with the bait of great promises, being told that they were going to a country where they should live like gentlemen; that they should ride in their coaches, with several negroes to attend them; that they should possess large plantations of their own, and soon be in a condition to come home and visit their friends with great pomp and grandeur. By these specious and artful insinuations, many unthinking giddy youths were seduced into slavery, relying on promises which were meant only to insnare and not to inrich them. Some were carried off from their parents by violence, and whipt into the flock, like strayed sheep going to the shambles. All these methods, and many more, were practiced in this execrable branch of traffick, of which the Reader will find a proof to his conviction, by perusing the depositions formerly inserted.

How far these specious promises were fulfilled, will appear from the treatment we met with when landed in America. On our arrival there, our merchant, or supercargo, who had the charge of us, took the earliest opportunity to dispose of us to the planters, some of whom will buy ten, others twenty, to labour in their plantations and cultivate their ground. Thus were we driven through the country like cattle to a Smithfield market, and exposed to sale in public fairs, as so many brute beasts. When thus maltreated by our countrymen, what reason had we to expect better usage from our new masters, whose property we now were? Luckily for me, I fell into the hands of one of my own countrymen, who had undergone the same fate himself, and who used me in a more tender manner than many of my companions in slavery had to boast of. No thanks, however, to my Kidnappers; for if the devil had come in the shape of a man to purchase us, with money enough in his pockets, it would have been as readily accepted as of the honestest and most humane man in the world. Besides, these children are sometimes sold to barbarous and cruel masters, from whom they often make an elopment, to avoid the harsh usage they daily meet with; but as there is scarce a possibility of making a total escape, they are generally taken and brought back, and for every day they have been absent, they are compelled to serve a week, for every week a month, and for every month a year; they are besides obliged to pay the cost of advertising, apprehending, and bringing them back, which often protracts their slavery four or five years longer. But a more shocking case often occurs; some of these poor deluded slaves, after groaning for some time under the yoke of tyranny and oppression, with only a distant prospect of relief, in order to put an end to their bondage, put a period to their lives at the same time. What a dismal reflection this, to be the instrument of driving an innocent helpless creature to despair, and ruining him both in soul and body!

The planters themselves are generally of an idle indolent disposition, not caring to fatigue themselves with work. How soon therefore they can raise 20 or 30 *l*. they purchase servants from the European merchants, whom they make slaves, some for four or five, others for seven years. These they send to the woods, or employ in other kinds of hard labour, and oblige them to perform a certain task of work in a day; in which if they fail, they are severely punished by their masters, who review their work at night. Nor dare the servant, when he is thus chastised, presume to vindicate himself, for fear of giving a new offence to this unrelenting tyrant, whose humour must be indulged, even at the expence of strokes and blows. This is generally the case throughout the different colonies in N. America; but more especially in Maryland and Virginia. These two are the best markets to which our European merchants can resort for the sale of their illicit cargoes of slaves. Here they may barter them for tobacco, the staple commodity of these colonies, upon which they have an immense return of profit.

The servants in Maryland are mostly convicts, who have been banished [from] their native country for misdemeanors; yet some of them, when their period of slavery is over, acquire plantations of their own, and are very expert in raising tobacco, and in the other branches of trade in that country. They frequently contract with their correspondents in Europe, to send them over men, women and children, to be employed in the culture of their plantations: But the fallacious promises of the undertakers here, are so pernicious to those whom they engage, that they generally prove their utter destruction. By their manner of cajoling, they induce those ignorant creatures to believe, that, when they indent themselves for four or five years, to serve in the plantations, they are to have high wages, to be paid annually as in their mother-country: But when these deluded persons come to make the experiment, they will find it quite the contrary. Be assured, you will meet with no such entertainment in any part of America; for you must serve your indented time, agreeable to the laws of the country, without one farthing of allowance, but at the discretion of your master; and it is well if you are furnished with cloaths sufficient to cover your nakedness.

Besides, you who indent yourselves in this manner, labour under another disadvantage; for, in that country, they are of opinion, (and a natural presumption it is) that when men and women, come to the age of maturity, willfully and deliberately agree to transport themselves as slaves for any number of years, they must have been guilty of some notorious crime; those, therefore, who come over in this manner, are looked upon as in the black class of convicts, who for fear of a prosecution at home, take this step to prevent a discovery of their vices. For some time, honest people who had engaged to serve in that country, suffered considerably on this account, both in their characters and fortunes, as these renegadoes were allowed to be evidences against them, and to swear away their reputations. But this has at last been debarred by the laws of the country, as none are allowed this privilege, unless they bring along with them a certificate, signed and attested by persons of character and repute, bearing that they were descended of honest parents, and that nothing criminal or dishonest can be laid to their charge; this being approved off [of] and recorded in the books of a court of Justice, the person's oath is then deemed legal.

From hence it appears, that numberless inconveniences and disadvantages attend the person, who, tho' of an age capable to dispose of himself, by foolishly listening to the deceitful promises of these recruiters for slaves, at once stakes his happiness, his liberty, and perhaps his life. You will perhaps be told that you are going to a country flowing with milk and honey. These, it is true, are to be had in great plenty in America; but before you come to enjoy them, you will find that you must wade thro' an ocean of labour and fatigue, and that out of the sweet cometh forth bitterness. Whereas, if you are possessed but of three or four pounds to pay your passage, and are of an ingenious disposition, whether in mechanicks, commerce, agriculture or manufactures, you are certain not only of handsome bread, but, by moderate frugality and industry, of making a genteel fortune in a few years.

Depositions of witnesses on the part of Peter Williamson.

ALEXANDER KING depones, That he knew the deceased James Williamson in Hirnley in the parish of Aboyne; That the said James

Williamson had a son, named Peter Williamson, whom the deponent knew when he was a boy; and he seeing the said Peter Williamson immediately at his emitting this deposition, he is very sure he's the identical Peter Williamson, whom he knew when he was a boy. Depones, That, some years before the battle of Culloden, and, so far as he remembers, he believes it was upwards of four years before the battle of Culloden, it was the general report of the country, that when the said Peter Williamson, the Pursuer, was a little boy, going with a clipped head, he was taken at Aberdeen, and carried to Philadelphia along with several other boys. Depones, That, about that time, the Deponent had a conversation with the said James Williamson concerning his son Peter, who told the Deponent several times, that he came into Aberdeen seeking his son Peter, but they would not let him near hand him. Depones, That the said James Williamson told the Deponent, that his son Peter was in custody in a barn at Aberdeen, and they would not let him speak to him; and afterwards the said James Williamson told the Deponent, that the merchants of Aberdeen had carried away his son to Philadelphia, and sold him for a slave. Depones, That he heard in the country by report, that John Elphingston merchant in Aberdeen, and one Black a merchant there, whether James or George he does not remember, did deal in that way of carrying away boys. And further depones, That the said James Williamson told him, the Deponent, that his son Peter was carried away without his consent, and he saw the father shed ma[n]y salt tears on that account.

JOHN WILSON depones, That he knew, and was well acquainted with James Williamson in Hirnley, and with all his children, particularly his son Peter Williamson. Depones, That the said Peter Williamson having gone to Aberdeen, as the Deponent was informed, he was caried away therefrom to the plantations; and when his father and friends missed him, they made search for him many ways in the country, but could not find him; and the said James Williamson went to Aberdeen in search of him, and, upon his return, he told the Deponent, that he had been at Aberdeen seeking his son Peter, but could not find him, and was informed that he was taken up at Aberdeen, and carried to the plantations. Depones, That he believes, when the said Peter Williamson was amissing, he was about eight or ten years of age, and was a stout boy; and the Deponent seeing the said Peter Williamson immediately at emitting this deposition, he is sure that he is the identical person whom he knew, before he went away, to be James Williamson's son, and was at the said Peter Williamson's baptism.

FRANCIS FRASER of Findrack, Esq; depones, That, about twenty years ago, he knew the deceased James Williamson living in Upper-Balnacraig, in the Parish of Lumphanan, and that he heard the said James Williamson lived formerly in Hirnley, in the parish of Aboyne. Depones, He knew several of the said James Williamson's children, and he heard it was the practice of some of the merchants in Aberdeen, to kidnap young children, and send them to the plantations to be sold for slaves. Depones, He heard in the country, that the said James Williamson or his wife, had gone into Aberdeen, and one of their sons called Peter Williamson had followed, and that James Smith sadler in Aberdeen had picked up the said Peter; and the Deponent heard he was either put in prison, or put on board a ship, till the ship sailed. Depones, It was the voice of the country, that James Williamson and his wife regreted or made a clamour for the loss of their son, not knowing what was become of him.

ROBERT REID depones, That, to the best of his remembrance, he came to Aberdeen in the year 1740, to see his sister; that his sister proposed to the Deponent to go to a barn, to see the country boys who were going over to Philadelphia, and to carry home to their parents some accounts of them; that the Deponent accordingly went over, and heard music and a great noise in said barn; but the Deponent refused to go in, because it occurred to him, that he had heard in his own country, that many other boys had been decoyed by particular artifices of merchants (and he has heard John Burnet named) to go over to America. Depones, That he was told that the number of boys in the said barn, was between thirty and forty. Depones, That, some time after this, the Deponent's mother refused to allow the Deponent to go into Aberdeen, and mentioned as the reason of this refusal, that the son of one Williamson, a tenant of Lord Aboyne's in Hirnley, and who lived within two miles of her, was amissing.

ISABEL WILSON depones, That she went to Aberdeen in the year 1740, and lived there for seven years and a half, and that she heard it frequently reported in Aberdeen, that many young people of both sexes were decoyed by the artifices of merchants in Aberdeen, particularly John Burnet and John Elphingston, to engage to go over to America. That she once went into a malt-barn to see one Peter Ley, who had engaged to go to America, and might be about thirty years of age: that, upon that occasion, she saw the barn full of boys and men, to the number of fifty and upwards, as she believes, and that they had a piper amongst them; and that particularly she saw two young boys called Elsmies, whom she knew, and who were the sons of a widow woman there; the youngest of whom appeared to her to be about ten years of age, and the eldest about fourteen years. Deposes, That after she left Aberdeen and went back to her own country, she has heard James Williamson, tenant of Lord Aboyne in the town of Hirnley, frequently complain, that a son of his had been a-missing, and he did know not what became of him.

MARGARET REID depones, That, about the year 1740, or 41, she heard that many young boys were decoyed by merchants in Aberdeen, particularly John Burnet, to go over to America, and that, about that time, one Peter Ley, and two brothers of the name of Elsmie, who lived in Aboyne, in the Deponent's neighbourhood, were a-missing, and were much regretted by their mother, and who were believed to have been carried over to America. Depones, That, in the parish of Aboyne, they were generally afraid to send their boys on errands to Aberdeen, for fear they should be carried off. Depones, That she did not know the age of the said two Elsmies, but from their appearance, the one might be ten or twelve, and the other seven or eight years. Depones, That James Williamson tenant in Hirnley of Aboyne, had a son who was a-missing, whose name was Peter, and who the Deponent knew very well at that time, and who, in the year 1740, might be nine or ten years of age, in the Deponent's opinion; that in that year he was sent into Aberdeen to be under his aunt's care, his mother being dead; That soon thereafter he was a-missing, and the Deponent has frequently heard his father regret him very much, who went into Aberdeen in search of him, but could not find him; and that it was the general opinion, of the country, and the opinion of his father also, that he was carried over to America.

GEORGE JOHNSTON depones, That he was sent over to Virginia by an uncle, to be put under the care of a friend there; that the ship in which he sailed was called the Indian Queen, Capt Ferguson commander; and the said ship sailed from Aberdeen, and had above sixty boys on board, under indentures to serve for a number or years in Virginia: That, as the Deponent has been frequently informed, many of these boys were engaged by different artifices to enter into the said indentures without the consent of their parents; and the Deponent particularly knows, that there were two brothers went over in the said ship, *to wit*, James and William Sheds, the eldest of whom was about fifteen years of age, and the other about six years; that these two brothers were bought by one John Graham, in Quantigo Creek in Virginia; that the eldest served out the time of his indenture, which was five years, and the youngest was adjudged to serve the said John Graham until he was twenty-one years of age. Depones, That he has been well informed, that James Abernethy, John Elphinston, and John Burnet, merchants in Aberdeen, were very much employed in engaging boys as aforesaid. Depones, That he knows that six or seven of the boys before-mentioned, were sold in Virginia to different masters; one of them, named Thomas Whitehead, was sold to the Deponent's master; that one of them called James Shed, the youngest of the two Sheds above mentioned, was sold to a planter within three miles of where the Deponent lived; that he deserted his master's service, was apprehended, and whipped for so doing, and adjudged to serve for a year longer than otherwise he was obliged to do, he having deserted his service for the space of a month. Depones, That he knows that in the year 1745, there came a ship from Aberdeen to Virginia, and that he was particularly acquainted with Thomas Whitehead abovementioned, who, upon recollection, he remembers came over a passenger in that ship, and not in the ship before mentioned: that the said Thomas Whitehead acquainted the Deponent, that he was engaged by James Abernethy merchant in Aberdeen, to go to Virginia to serve there. Depones, That the boys brought over as above, and engaged to serve in Virginia, are in use to be maintained by their masters during the time of their service; and at the end of their service to get 50 s. sterling, and have no other encouragement. Depones, That during their service, they are commonly very harshly used by their masters, and kept upon a very coarse diet, so that they are often forced to desperate measures, and to make away with themselves. Depones, That he returned to Britain in the end of the year 1745, and soon thereafter came to Aberdeen; and that there several of the parents of the children that had gone over with him, came to the Deponent, and with great anxiety enquired after their children; and particularly one Helen Law asked the Deponent about her son, and at the same time poured out a great many curses upon the said James Abernethy, for decoying young boys, and sending them to America, and particularly her own son; and that this she did in presence of the said James Abernethy. And depones, That the Deponent was sent down by his master along with John Spriggs, to bring up the said Thomas Whitehead, together with several others of the boys that came along with him, in order for sale. Depones, That he never saw the Pursuer [Peter Williamson] in Virginia, but has good reason to believe he was there, not only because some of his dearest relations had told him so, but that he himself had conversed particularly with him, with regard to several persons and places there, of which he gave a just and true account.

ALEXANDER GRIGERSON depones, That he and another boy (whose name he does not remember) were coming from the miln of Crathy, where they had been seeking their meat, and near to a birch wood near to the kirk of Crathy, three country men on horseback came up with them, but the Deponent knew none of them; and they asked the Deponent and the other boy that was along with him, if they would go with them, and they would clothe them like gentlemen, and said very kind things to them; but the Deponent, being elder than the other boy, made answer, That they would not go along with them; for it struck the Deponent in the head, that perhaps he and the other boy were to be carried abroad, in respect a rumour prevailed in the country, that young boys were carried abroad at that time, Depones, That upon their refusing to go along with the said three men, they said they would force them; and thereupon alighted from their horses; and while the said three men were tying their horses to growing trees, he, the Deponent, and the other boy run away into the wood, and hid themselves into a thick bush, and the three men followed them, but did not find them, though they passed by within three yards of them; and the Deponent heard one of them say, "Go you that way, and I shall go this way, and if we can find them in this bush, we can easily take them up." Depones, That he and the other boy stayed about half an hour in the bush, till they found that the said three men were gone away, and then he, the Deponent, and the other boy, went back to the miln of Crathy.

MARGARET ROSS depones, That, about 17 years ago, she had a son named James Ingram, then about twelve years of age, whom she sent an errand to Aberdeen, and who at that time was taken up by Alexander Gray merchant in Aberdeen, in order to be carried to the Plantations; that he was detained in Aberdeen about eight days, but had liberty to go through the town with other boys, and they used to go in companies beating the drum. Depones, that, on Sunday thereafter, she came to the chapel in the Gallowgate to hear worship, and she saw her son there, and got hold of him, and carried him home with her to Loan-head, which is about half a mile from Aberdeen. Depones, that she kept her said son at home for some time, until four men came out of Aberdeen for him, in the night time, while the Deponent and her husband were in bed, and their son James lying at their feet. Depones, she knew none of these four men, but they told they were come from the said Alexander Gray, and wanted to carry the said James Ingram into Aberdeen. Depones, that when her son heard them saying so, he wept and shed tears; and they insisting, caused him rise out of bed, and go along with them to Aberdeen, and his father followed them, and she was told by her husband, they went to Alexander Gray's house. Depones, that, next day, the said John Ingram, her husband, (as he informed the Deponent) came into Aberdeen, and met with Alexander Gray, and sought back his son; who said to him, That, if he would pay seven pounds Scots, for the expense of maintaining his son while he was with Alexander Gray, in that case he should get back his son; but their circumstances could not allow them to pay the said seven pounds. Depones, that thereafter she came into Aberdeen, and met with Provost Aberdeen, who was then provost of the town, and represented the case to him, and he sent for Alexander Gray to come to the town-house and speak with the provost. Depones, that when he came, the provost asked him if he had a boy of the Deponent's with him; to which Alexander Gray answered, that he had a boy, one James Ingram; whereupon the provost said to him, That he did not think it right to take up any person's child without consent of parents; to which Alexander Gray answered, that the boy complained that his mother was not good to him; and the provost replied, that a parent could not correct a child out of time, and desired, that the Deponent should get her son: whereupon Alexander Gray asked who would pay his charges for maintaining the boy while he had him; at same time Gray said, he had given off the boy to one Mr. Copland in the Gallowgate. Depones, that the provost sent an officer for Mr. Copland, who could not be found that day, but the provost desired the Deponent to go home, and return next day to the town-house, and she should get her son. Depones, that on her return, the provost sent for Mr. Copland, and ordered him to give the Deponent her son; and he asked who would pay the charges of him; and the provost replied, that when his father grew rich, he would cut stones for him, he being a stone-cutter to his employment. Depones, that Mr. Copland went along with her to a barn at the back side of the town, where her son and several other boys were, the door whereof was open, and James Ross, an officer standing thereat. Depones, that several of the boys came out of the barn calling to Mr. Copland for shoes, and other necessaries that they wanted, and her son came to the door to her, and Mr. Copland desired to take from him a stripped vest-coat that he had given him; which was taken from him accordingly, and the Deponent put a plaid about her son above his shirt, and carried him home with her. Depones, that she kept her son at home a considerable time with herself; thereafter he went into Aberdeen, and was taken up (as she was informed) by one Lunen in Aberdeen, who went over with boys, and her son, a trader to the Plantations. Depones, that, before her son went away, he was put into the tolbooth of Aberdeen, and kept there for several weeks by the said

Mr. Lunen; and the Deponent went twice or thrice to the tolbooth and saw her son there, and gave him her blessing before he went away, and she never saw him since. Depones, that when she went into Alexander Gray's shop, who caused first apprehend her boy, to seek him back, the said Alexander Gray took her by the shoulders and thrust her out of his shop. Depones, that, at the aforesaid time, when her son was taken up and carried away, provisions were very dear and scarce, and many were difficulted to get their bread; but the Deponent and her husband were in condition to have maintained her son, and never consented to his being carried off. ---- JOHN INGRAM depones conform to the said Margaret Ross his spouse.

WILLIAM JAMIESON depones, That in spring 1741, and for some years before and after, the Deponent resided with his family in the town of Old Meldrum, which he reckons to be twelve computed miles from Aberdeen: that the Deponent had a son named John, who was, in the spring of 1741, between ten and eleven years of age; that, about that time, the said John his son having been amissing from his house, the Deponent was informed by the neighbours in Old-Meldrum, the day after he was amissing, that they saw a man, whom they said was a servant to John Burnet, late merchant in Aberdeen, who was commonly called Bonny John, with the Deponent's said son, and two other boys much about the same age, travelling towards Aberdeen; and that his son would be sent to the plantations: That, in two or three days after receiving this information, the Deponent went to Aberdeen, where he found the said John Burnet, who told him that he had several boys, but did not know whether the Deponent's son was amongst them; but said, that though he was, the Deponent would not get him back, because he was engaged with him, that the Deponent upon this left Mr. Burnet, and went down about the shore, where he had been informed the boys were out getting the air; that when he came there, he observed a great number of boys, he thinks about sixty, diverting themselves; that they were attended by a man, who, the Deponent was informed by the people of the town, was employed for that purpose by the said John Burnet; that this man had a horse-whip, and the Deponent observed him striking the boys therewith when they went out of the croud. Depones, That he observed his own son John amongst these boys, and called upon him; that the boy came up to him, and told him that he would willingly go home with him if he was allowed; that immediately upon this, the person who was Mr. Burnet's overseer, came up and gave the boy a lash with his whip, and took him by the shoulder, and carried him amongst the rest, and immediately drove them off, and carried them to a barn, where the Deponent saw them locked in by the fore-mentioned overseer, who put the key in his pocket: that the place where the boys were standing when the Deponent spoke with his son as above-deponed on, was on the shore, and the Deponent thinks, as far distant from the fore-mentioned barn, as from the Writer's Court to the Nether-bow-port; that when the boys were marching up to the barn, the Deponent kept pace with the overseer, who followed immediately after the boys, intreating of him to get liberty to speak to his son; who answered him, that he should get leave to speak with him by and bye when they were come to the barn; but when they came there, the overseer locked the door as above-mentioned, and refused the Deponent access; that the Deponent in passing through the town of Aberdeen after his son was so locked up from him, was told by several trades people, and others to whom he had told the story of his son, that it would be in vain for him to apply to the magistrates to get his son liberate; because some of the magistrates had a hand in those doings, as well as the said John Burnet; upon which the Deponent went home. That in summer thereafter, the Deponent came up to Edinburgh to take advice what he should do in this matter, being certainly informed by the voice of the country, that the ship on board of which his son was put, had sailed for Maryland about a fortnight or so after that day when the Deponent was at Aberdeen, and saw his son as before-mentioned. That after the Deponent came up to Edinburgh, he was recommended to the deceased Mr. William Seton writer to the Signet[94], who gave him a libelled summons against the said John Burnet, before the Lords of Council and Session, for restitution of the Deponent's son; that none of the messengers in Aberdeen would execute the summons against Mr. Burnet, because they would not disoblige him for any thing the Deponent could give them; which obliged the Deponent to send a messenger from Old Meldrum to Aberdeen; that the Deponent having insisted in this summons, the said John Burnet applied to the late Earl of Aberdeen, who sent for the Deponent's father, his tenant; and the Deponent's father came and carried him to the house of Haddo, where the Earl and John Burnet were at that time; that, at this meeting, it was agreed, that the said John Burnet should give the Deponent his bond to restore his son to him within the space of a twelve month, under the penalty of 50 s. Sterling; that the Deponent, did not get the said bond, but that the Earl of Aberdeen promised that he would cause John Burnet grant the bond; that the Deponent thinks, to the best of his remembrance, this meeting was in the end of summer 1742; that shortly thereafter Lord Aberdeen died, and the Deponent having inlisted as a soldier, was sent over to

Flanders, where he served some years, and upon his return John Burnet was become bankrupt, and had left the country: and the Deponent knows not whether his son is dead or alive, having never heard of him since he was carried from Aberdeen, and never got the bond before-mentioned from John Burnet.

GEORGE LESLIE depones, That, about the year 1742, it was the current report, that Hugh Mackie stabler in Aberdeen, was employed by John Burnet merchant in Aberdeen for taking up boys, that they might be carried to the plantations. Depones, That the said Hugh Mackie, with a gang of five or six boys along with him, was at the back of the Gallowgate, where the Deponent was working as a mason's servant, and they observing a boy coming down the street, they took hold of him: but the boy struggled and got out of their grips; whereupon Hugh Mackie kicked the said boy with his foot, and turned him into the loch, and the boy being hurt, was confined in the house of Harry Black stabler for eight or ten days, till he recovered; but the Deponent does not know what became of that boy afterwards. Depones, That he saw a parcel of boys and girls confined in a barn in the Green, before they were sent to the plantations. Depones, That he believes they were of different ages, from ten to fifteen years.

CHRISTIAN FINLATER depones, That some years before the battle of Culloden, Hugh Mackie stabler in the Gallowgate of Aberdeen, and James Wilson stabler there, were employed for taking up boys to be sent to the plantations; and one time she saw the said Hugh Mackie driving a parcel of boys before him down the Gallowgate, with a staff in his hand, and she has seen him chasing boys in at closes. Depones, She saw some boys looking out at the window of a barn in the Green, and she reckons they were kept there till they should be sent to the plantations; and she heard there were other places in town where boys were kept until they should be sent away. Depones, That, according to her knowledge and belief, some of these boys would have been twelve years of age, others of them thirteen; and some above and some less; and she saw, among them, lads from the Highlands of the size of men, and women also; and the boys were generally strapping boys. Depones, That she heard one Mr. Copland in Aberdeen was concerned in employing Hugh Mackie and James Wilson for the above purpose.

ROBERT BRAND depones, That about the month of June 1758, he the Deponent saw James Thomson Dean of Guild's officer, carrying out of George Mackie's house (where Peter Williamson was quartered at that time) a parcel of books, bound or stitched in blue paper; the Deponent does not know the number of them, but James Thomson had his arms extended full of them. Depones, That thereafter he saw a servant-maid of George Mackie's coming down stairs of Mr. Mackie's house, after the town-officer had come out of it, and the Deponent asked her what was the matter; and she answered, that it was the town-officers carrying away Mr. Williamson's books to the clerk's-chamber, where Mr. Williamson was himself, and this was the second burden of them.

GEORGE MACKIE depones, That two or three of the town-officers came to the Deponent's own house, and he saw them carry away all the copies of the said pamphlets or books, and the said Peter Williamson was along with the officers, and they were carried to the Town-house. Depones, That he saw some of these copies drop by the way as the officers were carrying them to the Town house, but he does not know how many copies were so dropped, neither did he see Peter Williamson take up any of the dropt copies. Depones, That, when Peter Williamson was appointed by the Magistrates to find bail for his appearance to stand trial on the complaint against him, at the instance of the Dean of Guild and Procurator-fiscal, and when he was put in prison till he should find the said bail; he the said Peter Williamson sent for the Deponent to speak to him and to bail him: Accordingly the Deponent came up the Tolbooth-stair, and found him confined in that part of the prison opposite to the door of the Court-room, and the Deponent spoke to the said Peter Williamson through the bars of the door of the place where he was confined; and that the said Peter Williamson desired the Deponent to become bail for him, and he the Deponent became bail for his appearance before the Magistrates, and he thinks he signed something for that purpose, and thereupon the said Peter Williamson was set at liberty; and the Deponent had him over to his house, and presented him before the Magistrates next day. Depones, That, after the magistrates had pronounced sentence against the said Peter Williamson, he came over to the Deponent's house, and told the Deponent that he had been threatened to sign a paper, obliging himself to go out of the town, and that if he did not sign the paper, he was threatened to be again imprisoned; thereafter, the said Peter Williamson hurried himself away out of the Deponent's house in less than a quarter of an hour, leaving behind him some of his baggage, which he desired to be sent after him to Newcastle, and which the Deponent sent to him accordingly. Depones, that he was an inhabitant of Aberdeen from the year 1740, and that about the year 1741 downward to the year 1744, it was a custom for several of the merchants of Aberdeen, to carry on a trade of transporting young boys and women to the Plantations, of different ages. Depones, That he knew the persons after-named were concerned in that way of trade, *viz* George Garioch, John Elphingston, John Burnet, Alexander Gray, Lewis Gordon and Andrew Logie, all merchants in Aberdeen, and James Smith sadler there.

JAMES RATTARY, depones, That some more than three years ago, the Pursuer, Peter Williamson, was in Aberdeen, and being carried before the Magistrates by the town officers, the Deponent, as he understood Peter Williamson was a stranger, having been several times in company with him before that day, he went into the court house, where he heard the clerk and some of the Magistrates, but cannot particularly say which of them, challenge the said Peter Williamson for selling and distributing the pamphlet libelled, reflecting upon the merchants of Aberdeen as Kidnappers, and that they used very rough language to the said Peter Williamson, but he does not remember the expressions, not having given great attention thereto, at least, the expressions have now escaped his memory. Depones, That before the Deponent left the court, he saw the Pursuer carried off by the town-officers by order of the court, but knows not where they carried him to, further than that next day, or the day thereafter, the Deponent happening to be in the house of George Mackie inn-keeper, he was informed by the said George Mackie, that Peter Williamson was obliged to leave the town; and that he, the said George Mackie had become bail to present him to the Magistrates any time within six months, under a penalty; and that both Mackie and his wife said to the Deponent, that he had been very ill used by the magistrates.

Depositions on the part of the Magistrates.

GEORGE GARIOCH merchant in Aberdeen, depones, that about the year 1740, and forward for some years, several of the gentlemen merchants in Aberdeen, were in use to indent servants for America; and if any young boys or girls of under-age, were so indented, and that any of their parents or relations came to claim them back, even after they were indented and attested, they were, so far as the Deponent knows or remembers, delivered back to their parents or relations, upon paying up what money the merchant had debursed on their account. Depones, That he was informed, that, unless a servant was attested,[95] their indentures were of no avail, and which was his own opinion. Depones, That several servants were indented in the years 1740 and 1741, at which time provisions were scarce in this country; that many servants were turned off from their masters, who could not afford them daily bread for their work, which forced sundry persons to come from the country to Aberdeen and indent; and on that account, the Deponent himself at that period indented several out of charity, and, for the above reasons, believes he was the first, at that time of scarcity, that began to indent such servants. And being interrogate by the said Peter Williamson, whether or not he employed people to go and inlist such kind of servants through the country; or if all the servants he inlisted about that period, came to the Deponent's house voluntarily, to be indented by him? Depones, That he never employed persons to go and bring persons to be indented as servants at his house, but such as he indented came of themselves, or with their companions, voluntarily to him, and that some of those who had indented, he has afterwards discharged, without exacting any money of them. And being further interrogate by the said Peter Williamson, whether or not there were any boys or children from eight to fourteen years of age that indented themselves with the Deponent, or did their parents after they were indented, come and demand them back from you after they were indented? or did you not send over boys of that age, after they desired themselves to be released, or that their parents or relations had come and demanded them back? and were any of such young boys or children offered up by their parents or relations to you to be indented for scarcity of bread, who were to your knowledge the masters of such servants, who dismissed them as before said? and whether or not did you sell such indented boys in America; for what number of years, and what sums did you receive for them? Depones, That he never indented any boy or girl of eight or ten years of age, except when the parents of such children indented with him likewise. Depones, That he never sent off any boys or girls of under-age indented with him, that had been demanded back by their parents or friends. Depones, That never did he indent any boys or girls in town, without their parents consent. Depones, That several servants were indented as aforesaid by the Deponent, who told the Deponent they were turned off by their masters for want of bread, but does not remember the names of their masters. Depones, That he went not to America himself, but that their indentures were sold there from 5 *l.* to 8 *l.* Sterling; that such as were under age might be indented for five or six years, and such as were of full age, only for four.

ALEXANDER GORDON ship-master in Aberdeen depones, That it has been a practice for to indent servants to be carried from Aberdeen to the Plantations in America, from the year 1735 downward to the year

1753; and that, during the foresaid period, he has been concerned himself in that trade of indenting, for his own account and of his owners, servants from Aberdeen, and carrying them over to the American Plantation, in different ships commanded by him on different voyages, *viz.* in the brig Diligence, to Philadelphia, and the Ruby, to Virginia and Maryland. Depones, That he has carried over boys, but not under fourteen years of age, to continue [no?] longer than the servants attain the age of twenty-one years, by the custom of Maryland; and that the price he generally received for such servants in Maryland and at Philadelphia, amounted to about 10 *l.* Sterling over-head.

ALEXANDER GRAY merchant in Aberdeen depones, That it was a custom nineteen or twenty years ago, and since, that several merchants in the town of Aberdeen, were in practice of hiring boys, girls, and other servants, attested before the magistrates of Aberdeen, or some other Justice of Peace, to be carried to America, or other of his Majesty's Plantations, to be disposed of there. *Causa scientiae* [the cause of knowledge], the Deponent dealt in that way himself.

HELEN LAW depones, That about the years 1740, 1741, 1742, and since, several of the merchants of Aberdeen were in practice to inlist boys to be indented, to carry over as servants to the plantations, *viz.* George Black, Alexander Gray, George and Andrew Gariochs, Mr. Copland, James Abernethy, John Elphingston, all merchants in Aberdeen, and Capt Robert Ragg ship-master, and James Smith sadler there; and that these several merchants have employed the Deponent to furnish diet to boys and servants that had indented with them: Depones, That about seventeen years past the month of May last, the Deponent was employed to furnish diet to a parcel of boys and servants that were afterwards carried over from Aberdeen to the plantations by the said Captain Robert Ragg. Depones, That there were nine of the young boys whom she dieted at that time, that were never confined, but that several of the big boys and men who were threatening to run off, that were afterwards confined in prison, or in the work-house of Aberdeen, for some short time before Captain Ragg sailed. Depones, That among the boys that were never confined, and dieted at her house, there was one boy named Peter M'William, who would have been upwards of twelve years of age, a long stowie clever boy, (by which she means a growthie boy). Depones, That these boys came not all at one time to diet with her; she began with some of them a little after Martinmas, and they were continuing to come to her till within a day or two before the sailing of the ship in May thereafter;

and that their weekly board was twenty pence a week for each, and that the boy Peter M'William was some weeks dieted by her. Depones, That there were four or five of those boarded with her that were delivered back by the merchants to their friends, on paying the charges they had cost the merchants. Depones, That for five weeks before the ship commanded by Capt. Robert Ragg sailed from the harbour of Aberdeen, she lay at the key of Tory, and the boys were carried over to the ship; during which space the Deponent went over and hired a house at Tory, in which house she made their diet, and carried it to them on board the said ship during the space; and the Deponent was informed, that the reason why the ship lay at Tory, was that she was neeped, and had not water to carry her over the bar. And being further interrogate, If Peter Williamson, whom she now sees before her, is the identical person that dieted at the time foresaid with her, then named Peter M'William? Depones, That she cannot swear that he is the same person, for several of these boys returned from the plantations a few years after whom she did not know again when she saw them, by reason of the change in that time. Depones, that she had a son of her own that the year before had been carried over by James Abernethy merchant in Aberdeen, whom she had asked back, and Mr. Abernethy agreed at three different times to deliver him back to her, but he was resolute to go, and went accordingly. And being interrogate by the said Peter Williamson, whether or not the Deponent was not always in use to ask leave of the keepers on board of the ship, for the boys to come ashore any time when they lay at Tory, and such liberty was only obtained on the said Helen Law's obliging her to return them back on shipboard? Depones, that she did ask leave of the keepers on board of the ship for some of the said boys to come ashore with her, which she accordingly obtained, and did become bound to return them back to the ship, and on her verbal obligement or promise, she was allowed to bring some of them even over to the town of Aberdeen with her, and always returned them again on ship-board. Depones, That she knows nothing about their parents consenting to their indentures, as some might have had parents and some of them none, and severals of them were begging their bread through the town. But depones, That when any of their parents and relations claimed them, they were given them by the merchants on paying their charges.

JAMES ROBERTSON stabler in Aberdeen, depones, That about seventeen years past the month of May last, the Deponent was employed by James Smith sadler as keeper of several young boys, the youngest of whom would have been about ten years of age, and some of them sixteen and upwards, who were indented, and their indentures attested by the Magistrates of Aberdeen, to be carried over to the plantations in America, along with other servants, both men and women of full age, also indented and attested by the Magistrates of Aberdeen, to be shipped on board a ship lying at the harbour of Aberdeen, then commanded by Capt. Robert Ragg shipmaster in Aberdeen, and which ship was carried over to Tory, where she lay and received the said boys on board of her. The Deponent was sometime afterwards employed by the said James Smith to go over and stay on board the said ship as a keeper of the said boys and other servants, to the best of his remembrance for the space of twelve or fourteen days, till the ship sailed, and he went with them in said ship out of the harbour, till the ship was in the road before Aberdeen, from whence he returned back to the town of Aberdeen. Depones, That during the time the said James Robertson was on ship-board as above, there was also another keeper named Robert Adam along with him, employed likewise to take care of the said boys and servants. Depones, That all the night they were confined, and put to their beds in the hold of the ship, but all day had liberty to go upon the deck, and even to play them ashore, their keepers always looking after them, and some of them allowed to go to Helen Law's house to help her on board with victuals for themselves and others. Depones, That among the boys under the Deponent's and the other keeper's care, there was a boy of about fourteen years of age, who was called Peter M'William. Depones, That Peter Williamson, whom he sees presently before him, is the same person that was then named Peter M'William, as he presently apprehends, but will not swear positively that he is the same person; for that Peter M'William had black brows, and was pock-marked, and so is Peter Williamson whom he now sees; but does not remember any boy then aboard called Peter Williamson; and that Peter M'William was a stout, clever, rough loun, and very ill to guide.

JAMES SMITH sadler in Aberdeen, depones, That, to the best of the Deponent's memory, about nineteen or twenty years ago, but cannot be absolutely positive about the precise time, he was employed by John Elphingston merchant in Aberdeen, and Captain Robert Ragg shipmaster in Aberdeen, and Mr. Walter Cochran town-clerk-depute of Aberdeen, in partnership with them, to make leather-caps, and pay for diet, and to pay taylors for cloathing furnished to several young boys and other servants, that had entered into indentures, attested before the Magistrates of Aberdeen, with the above-named Captain Robert Ragg, to be carried from Aberdeen to America, to be disposed of at Philadelphia. Depones, That he accordingly furnished the said servants with leather caps, and paid for their cloathing and diet, for all which he was afterwards repaid by the above-named gentlemen. Depones, That, among them servants that were so indented, there was one boy named Williamson of about 12 years of age, and another boy of the same surname, of about 13 or 14 years of age, to the best of the Deponent's knowledge and remembrance; but depones, he does not know any of the said two boys Christian names. Depones, That he has not in his custody any accounts or writings relative to the servants that were sent from Aberdeen to the Plantations in the year 1743: But depones, that the account shewn to him at deponing, and exhibited by Walter Cochran town clerk depute of Aberdeen, consisting of twelve leaves, with a docquet on the last page thereof, dated 26th July 1743, is a just and true account, all wrote with the Deponent's hand writing; and the Deponent received from the said Walter Cochran payment of the balance of said account, conform to his receipt and discharge; and the whole of the articles in said account, and names therein insert, are genuine and true as wrote by the Deponent, and which account is signed by the Deponent and Commissioner at deponing. Depones, He heard the ship the Planter, Captain Robert Ragg master, who carried servants for the Plantations in the year 1743, was stranded on Cape May.

WALTER COCHRAN town-clerk-depute of Aberdeen, depones, and produces an account, wrote book-ways, and bound in marled paper, intitled, Account Bailie William Fordyce and Company to James Smith, which account begins the third day of December 1742, and consists of twelve leaves, and upon the last page thereof is a discharge by James Smith, dated the 26th July 1743, granting the receipt from the Deponent of payment of the balance of 18 *l.* 14 *s.* 5 *d.* Sterling, being full and complete payment of the above and foregoing accounts; and therefore discharging the Deponent and Company of all he could demand of them; upon the second page of which account, there is charged a six-pence for a pair of stockings to Peter Williamson, and five pence for a woollen cap to ditto, as deburshed 8th January 1743; and on the third page, there is charged one shilling and three-pence Sterling, for five days board of Williamson, as deburshed 13th January 1742. Depones, That he received the foresaid account from James Smith sadler in Aberdeen, and paid him the balance contained in the foresaid account, and which account is signed by the Deponent and Commissioner, and produced with the report; and further adds, that the foresaid account has been lying by the Deponent for several years past, he being one of the company that were owners of the ship the Planter, Robert Ragg master, who transported servants to the Plantations, and was wrecked at Cape May.

WILLIAM GIBSON carpenter in Tory, depones, That, before the 12th day of May 1743, the Deponent was hired as ship-carpenter to Captain Robert Ragg, to sail a voyage from Aberdeen to Virginia, on board his ship called the Planter, and that there were shipped a number of boys, girls, and other servants, under indenture, as he heard; but that in their voyage their ship was stranded on Cape May; but, some time after, all the servants they carried over were safely recovered, and a sloop came down from Philadelphia, and carried all of them up there.

JOHN DICKSON mariner in Stonehive, depones, That the Deponent, to the best of his remembrance, was engaged as a sailor in the year 1743, to serve under Captain Ragg, to navigate his ship called the Planter, from Aberdeen for Virginia. Depones, That the said ship, on her arrival from London, in order to perform the said voyage, lay at the pier of Tory until she sailed from said river on her voyage, as the Deponent remembers, on the 12th of May 1743, and took in her cargo there, which consisted of some parcels of goods, and several servants, being men, women, and boys, who, he believes, were all indented as servants, for behoof of the contractors with them, to be disposed of in Virginia: That the ship was, before her arrival, stranded to the northward of Cape May, upon a little island in the province of New Jersey, where she became a wreck. Depones, That how soon the ship struck, so many of the crew took out a yoal to discover a landing place, and the rest of the crew, and some of the servants went into the long-boat, and got safe ashore; and some of them returned with the long-boat, and brought out the rest of the servants; and afterwards a sloop came down very soon and carried them up to Philadelphia.

A Short HISTORY of the PROCESS between PETER WILLIAMSON and the Magistrates of Aberdeen.[96]

IN the Introduction to the former discourse on Kidnapping, I fairly stated the case betwixt the Magistrates of Aberdeen and me, without disguising the truth in any the most minute particular. I therefore appeal to the unbiassed judgment of the candid Reader, whether, after the unmerited maltreatment I suffered from the arbitrary proceedings of these Magistrates, merely for relating a simple, but disagreeable fact, I say, I submit it, whether I was not entitled to sue for redress before a higher tribunal. The motives or principles upon which they acted in the irregular prosecution against me, in which they were both my Accusers and Judges, I shall not pretend to determine; but from the proof before inserted, the Reader will hardly be at a loss to form a conjecture. In order to ascertain the power of a Magistracy, it is necessary to have recourse to the original institution of it. That liberty which the constitution of this country considers as its favourite object, is the result of the equipoise which our laws have established between the authority of Magistrates and the rights of the people. As the relative duties of Society must be inforced by the Magistrate, and compliance with the laws exacted from the citizens, by means of his authority, all the power that is necessary for these salutary purposes, is vested in him, and, in the due execution of it, he is not only intitled to the protection of the laws, but is an object of its veneration: Yet the same principles that have thus armed him with authority for the benefit of society, have wisely imposed upon him a restraint from abusing it. Sensible that authority improperly used, may become the most dreadful instrument of oppression, the law has not only declared wilful malversation in office to be a crime, but to those who have suffered by the proceedings of Magistrates, whether thro' inattention or ignorance (for ignorance is never blameless in a Magistrate), it has given an action of oppression and damages, for reparation of the injury the private party has suffered.

In this light did I consider the harsh sentence of the Magistrates of Aberdeen against me. Had they acted, according to the established forms of all courts of Justice, their proceedings would, at least, have had some colour of regularity; tho' their sentence would not have been less iniquous. Why was not I complained of by a party having interest in the cause? Why was not the complaint served upon me, and I appointed to give in Answers? Why were not the legal *induciae*, or days, allowed me to prepare for my defence? All these forms were neglected or despised. The Magistrates themselves instigated the complaint; they proceeded to judge upon it without service; without allowing *induciae* [time to prepare], and without answers. It is evident, therefore, they acted not as Magistrates, but as private oppressors.

Banished from the capital of the county wherein I was born, and stript of my all, I now bethought myself where or how to apply for redress. In this view I pursued my journey to Edinburgh; but, ignorant of the law, and unacquainted with any of its members, equally destitute of money and friends, and labouring under the reflections which the calumnious advertisement published by the Magistrates threw on my character, I was utterly at a loss to whom or in what manner I should apply for direction. From this dilemma, however, I was soon relieved by the assistance of kind providence, who threw me in the way of a Gentleman[97] versant in the Law, a Gentleman of knowledge, character and integrity by whose advice I was conducted, and by whose interest I was supported from the infancy to the conclusion of my Process. On a fair relation of my grievances, the injuries I suffered appeared to him so flagrant, that he did not hesitate a moment to declare his opinion, That I was not only entitled to ample damages from my prosecutors, but that the Court of Session would find no difficulty to award these, with full costs of suit. It is unnecessary here to take up the Reader's time in running over minutely the different steps of the Process from the beginning. Suffice it to say, that a Process of Oppression and Damages was commenced at my instance against the Magistrates of Aberdeen, wherein the Lord Ordinary allowed both parties a proof of the fact alledged on either side. And accordingly a Proof was taken, partly at Edinburgh, and partly at Aberdeen, of which the Reader has seen a specimen in the preceeding pages. I shall only observe here, that my personal presence being necessary on this occasion at the last mentioned place, I set out from Edinburgh for Aberdeen in September 1760, and tho' I had not the least knowledge of or connection with any single evidence I might bring, yet the trade of Kidnapping was so flagrant in that country, and had left such an impression on the minds of the people, that I was under no difficulty to bring a complete proof of the practice, by a number of persons who had suffered by it in being deprived of their children.

And here I cannot forbear doing justice to the conduct of the Gentleman whom I named as Commissioner, to take the depositions of the witnesses on the part of my Opponents. During the various steps of procedure in leading the Proof, wherein I met with all the obstructions that the malice of my enemies could throw in my way, he acted a most candid and ingenuous part.

After a short dependence, the Cause at last came to be advised in course before the Court of Session, by Memorials on the Proof; when, after hearing of parties at the bar at full length, their Lordships were pleased, on the 2d February 1762, to pronounce the following Interlocutor:

"The Lords having advised the state of the process, testimonies of the witnesses adduced, writs produced, with the memorials given in *hinc inde* [reciprocally], and having heard parties procurators thereon, find the libel relevant and proven; and find the defenders, conjunctly and severally, liable to the Pursuer in damages, and modify the same to the sum of 100 *l*. Sterling, and decern; and find the Defenders also, conjunctly and severally, liable to the Pursuer in the expences of this process, and of the extract of the Decreet, as the same shall be certified by the Collector of the clerk's fees; for which the Lords declare the Defenders to be personally liable, and that the same shall be no burden upon the town of Aberdeen; and ordain an account of the said expences to be given in; and ordain the accompt-book mentioned in the State,[98] and produced upon oath by Walter Cochran, and signed by the Lord President of this date, to remain in the hands of the clerk of this process, till further order of the Court[.]"

Against this Interlocutor the Magistrates presented a reclaiming Petition, craving either to be assoilzied [acquitted] from the Process; or, at least, that the damages awarded should be modified. To this Petition is subjoined the following curious letter.

Copy of a letter from William Davidson *and* James Jopp, *late Bailies of* Aberdeen, *to* Walter Scot *Writer to the Signet.*[99]

"SIR,

Aberdeen, February 4, 1762.

WE are very sorry to find, by yours of 30th past, that there is a sentence pronounced against us in Williamson's process, whereby we are decerned to pay him a very large sum out of our private pockets.

We think it necessary to inform you, that our conduct and intentions, with regard to our sentence against him, have been entirely misunderstood. We can with the greatest integrity declare, That, at the time of pronouncing that sentence, neither of us knew directly or indirectly, that Walter Cochran, the depute-clerk, was any wise concerned in transporting boys to America, or that there ever was in being the book he produced in the proof: That neither of us had ever any interest or concern in such trade: That we never knew, and did not believe, that any men or boys were ever transported from Aberdeen to American contrary to law: That we considered the paragraph in Williamson's pamphlet, respecting the merchants of Aberdeen, to be a very calumnious and reproachful aspersion on them which they did not deserve: That Williamson himself had the appearance of being an idle stroller, and could give no good account of himself, and had procured this pamphlet to be composed for him, of such shocking circumstances, in order the more easily to impose upon and draw money from the credulous vulgar: And, upon the whole, That we had no motive of interest, either on our own account, or any other person whatever, nor any prejudice against Williamson, (having never before seen or heard of him), to induce us to pronounce the sentence against him: That we did it purely as what we judged material justice, to vindicate the character of those we believed to be innocent, and were unjustly reflected upon; and that whatever in the sentence appears to their Lordships to be either oppressive or illegal, proceeded entirely from error in judgment, and not from any sinister design: So that however far the sentence has been wrong, we are ready most freely to make any declaration that may be necessary, that it proceeded from the most innocent intention.

Under these circumstances, you will easily perceive, how much we were surprised on reading yours, giving account of the sentence against us, and how hard a thing it is to be decerned to pay a sum of money as a fine, for doing what we considered to be our duty.

You will therefore lay this before the lawyers, in order they may the better form a reclaiming petition. We must think our case very hard, if their Lordships don't grant us redress in this matter. We are, &c.

W. DAVIDSON
JAMES JOPP."

This letter, however, did not avail their cause. It was in vain to deny their being in the knowledge that such an illicit species of traffick was carried on by some of the merchants in Aberdeen, when it was done in so public a manner, that the meanest residenter in the city observed it; when the *fama clamosa* [notorious rumor] of KIDNAPPING overspread the whole country, so that the poor people, whose business led them frequently to town, were afraid to carry their children along with them, least they should be pick'd up, and transported to the plantations. In the end they insinuate that their sentence against me proceeded from an error in judgment, and not from any sinister design, and that they were willing to make any declaration necessary, to evince the innocence of their intentions. But if a sentence calculated for the suppression of truth, and to prevent the detection of a commerce the most illegal and most destructive of Society, can be said to proceed from no sinister design, then every sentence that has a tendency to screen the guilty, and encourage those monsters who make a traffick of the persons and liberties of their fellow-creatures, must be accounted innocent. The whole of the procedure of the Magistrates against me, appears to have been directed to this single end. From this view, they *first* caused the whole impression of my book to be seized, and those offensive tell-truth leaves to be burnt, that they might not revive the memory of this villainous trade, and rise in judgment against their brother Merchants. *2do*, In order to make the surer work of it, they extorted from me the declaration inserted, *p.* 71–72 under the terror of imprisonment; and caused publish the same in the News-papers, in order to stigmatize my character, and brand me with the infamy of being an Impostor and a Liar. And, *lastly*, They banished me the city, least I should retract my declaration, and have an opportunity to spread the truth of my former assertions. Their schemes, however, had an effect the very reverse of what they intended. Instead of suppressing the truth, their proceedings have proved the means of bringing it to light, and confirming it by indubitable evidence: and so opening a scene of the grossest impiety, barbarity and wickedness.

To the above Reclaiming Petition, Answers were given in on my part, and the Lords, after re-considering the merits of the cause, were pleased to adhere to their former Interlocutor. Thus ended this process of oppression, carried on by a poor man, against the Magistracy of one of the most opulent and most respectable boroughs in Scotland.

It is the peculiar happiness of this land of liberty to be blessed with a Supreme Court, wherein justice is dispensed with an equal hand to the poor and rich; wherein the cause of the King and the Beggar is weighed in the balance of equity and law, and decided in favours of him whose scale preponderates. Happy is that nation whose Judges are men of integrity, uninfluenced by power, unbiass'd by party, and untainted by corruption! Such become the Guardians of the liberties and properties of the people, the protectors of the innocent, the scourges of the guilty, the supporters of the weak, and the terrors of the tyrant and oppressor. Such are the members of that honourable tribunal to which I appealed my cause, who redressed my grievances, and allowed me such compensation for those acts of violence and oppression which I had suffered from my tyrannical prosecuters, as they, in their wisdom, thought just and equitable. Nor must I omit to pay a tribute of gratitude to those worthy and learned Gentlemen who appeared in my cause at the bar, and who nobly exerted themselves in opening up and displaying that scene of oppression and lawless persecution wherewith I had been harrassed, and that without any prospect of fee or reward. In particular I must acknowledge my obligations to that learned Lawyer who was assigned me as Council by their Lordships, when my circumstances could not afford the price of a consultation. He generously embarked in my cause, and, by the force of argument, law and eloquence, exposed the injustice done me, and the weakness of my Opponent's reasonings, in such a light, that my plea became as clear as noon-day, and obvious to the meanest capacity.

    I shall trouble the Reader no further on this subject, my chief intent in publishing this narrative of my Process being, to warn Gentlemen in power and station, not to abuse them by a lawless exercise of their authority against the poor and innocent; for they may be assured, that power will not sanctify oppression, nor will justice be hood wink'd by riches. On the other hand, the weak and friendless need not despair of obtaining redress, though groaning under the yoke of tyranny: Let them have but the resolution to apply to the College of Justice; Providence will throw friends in their way, their oppressors shall hide their heads, and the cruelties they have committed be retaliated upon them.

    FINIS.

Endnotes

1. In the first edition of *French and Indian Cruelty*, Williamson claimed that he was eight years old at the time he was kidnapped. When the baptismal record he secured to prove his identity revealed that he had been thirteen years old at the time he sailed to America, he changed the wording of this passage to "under the years of pupillarity," or younger than fourteen.
2. Testimony in Williamson's lawsuits against the magistrates and merchants of Aberdeen told a different story about his kidnapping than the version presented here. His mother died sometime around 1740; not long afterward, his father lost his farm and the family fell on hard times. When pressed to identify the name or address of the aunt he supposedly lived with in Aberdeen, Williamson failed to reply. Testimony also indicated that Williamson and other servants recruited for the *Planter* were housed in a barn in the city before boarding the ship and that once there, they spent their days on deck and occasionally in town.
3. Cape May, New Jersey.
4. Williamson's account of the shipwreck is corroborated by several sources. According to customs records in Aberdeen, the *Planter* sailed for Maryland on May 13, 1743. Approximately eleven weeks later, the July 28, 1743 edition of the *Pennsylvania Gazette* noted that a ship from Aberdeen had recently come aground at Cape May. On September 1, 1743, another notice appeared in the same newspaper advertising "A Parcel of Scots SERVANTS" for sale by an owner intending "to leave the Province soon."
5. Tax records from the 1740s in Radnor Township in Chester County, Pennsylvania (approximately fourteen miles west of Philadelphia) identify a "Hugh Willson" as a farmer there. The tax lists are available in a searchable database from the Chester County Archives and can be found online at <www.chesco.org/archives>. Evidence supports Williamson's claim that his master had also been kidnapped into servitude. St. Johnstone is a place name associated with Perth. During the 1690s, eighty-three children from that region of Scotland who arrived in Philadelphia were brought before the Chester County Court of Quarter Session to have the length of their indentures determined. Included among them was "Hugh Woolson," judged to be twelve years of age and assigned a term of nine years. See *Collections of the Genealogical Society of Pennsylvania, volume 99: Court Records, Chester County, Penna., 1681–1697* (Philadelphia: GSP, 1921), section two, 4.

6. Williamson plagiarized this description of Philadelphia from the autobiographical narrative of Bampfylde-Moore Carew, another stroller active in eighteenth-century Britain who claimed to have spent time in North America as a transported felon. See C. H. Wilkinson (ed.), *The King of the Beggars: Bampfylde-Moore Carew* (Oxford: Clarendon Press, 1931), 196–8.
7. Williamson fabricated Wilson's bachelorhood and generous bequest to him. According to the Register of Wills in Philadelphia, Hugh Wilson died sometime between July 1748 and February 1749. He left the bulk of his estate to his wife, children, and grandchildren. There is no bequest mentioned for Williamson or any other servants. See "Last Will and Testament of Hugh Willson ... of Radnor in the County of Chester" in the Register of Wills Office in Philadelphia's City Hall, Room 185, in Will Book G (1743–1748/49), 325. An abstract of the will may be found in *Abstracts of Philadelphia County, Pennsylvania Wills, 1726–1747* (Westminster, MD: Family Line Publications, 1995), 171.
8. Williamson fabricated the story of his marriage and frontier homestead. He never names his wife or father-in-law in his narrative, nor did he ever name them after his return to Britain. There is no mention of the marriage or homestead in the relevant marriage, land, and taxation records of the era.
9. Williamson borrowed his description of the Indians' war cry from William Douglass, *A Summary, historical and political, of the first planting, progressive Improvements, and present State of the British settlements in North-America* 2 volumes (Boston: Rogers and Fowle, 1749–1751), 1:191–2. He likely consulted the London edition published in 1755.
10. The place names Williamson cites in his narrative indicate his familiarity with the geography of colonial Pennsylvania.
11. The names of other captives and torture victims that Williamson gives in his account of his captivity do not appear in any other contemporary sources describing the Indian war that engulfed Pennsylvania's frontier between 1755 and 1758. Williamson appears to have fabricated these individuals and incidents.
12. Thomas Kitchin's *A Map of the Province of Pensilvania*, published in the December 1756 edition of the *London Magazine*, located the Great Swamp in northeastern Pennsylvania, between the Delaware and Susquehanna Rivers. This map likely served as the source for several place names in Williamson's description of his captivity.
13. Conococheague Creek is a tributary of the Potomac River that runs through modern south central Pennsylvania. Scots Irish migrants settled in this valley in the generation before the Seven Years War.
14. There is no evidence of an Indian town named Alamingo in the Susquehanna Valley or elsewhere along the Pennsylvania frontier. Williamson likely borrowed the name from Allemangel, a town founded by German settlers in Pennsylvania's Northampton County that was attacked by Indians in 1756.

15. Many authors of captivity narratives inserted ethnographic observations about Native American culture—their dress and housing, their diet, their methods of warfare, their dances and celebrations—to lend authenticity to their stories. In Williamson's case, some of these details are so outlandish—such as the use of children to execute the elderly and the burial of the dead in standing positions—that they appear to be sensationalized figments of his imagination rather than information he may have culled from other oral or written sources.
16. French soldiers built Fort Duquesne in 1753, at the site where the Allegheny and Monongahela Rivers meet to form the Ohio (modern Pittsburgh, Pennsylvania). It was the major supply point for French-allied Indians who warred against the mid-Atlantic colonies from 1755 to 1758.
17. Pennsylvania's Blue Hills, also known as the Blue Mountains, range in a southwesterly arc from the Delaware Valley to the Maryland border, bisected by the Susquehanna River near modern Harrisburg.
18. The story Williamson tells of his escape shares elements in common with a captivity narrative published while he was serving as a soldier in North America. *A Narrative of the Suffering and Surprizing Deliverances of William and Elizabeth Fleming* (Philadelphia, 1756) tells the story of a husband and wife taken captive in Pennsylvania. Williamson may have borrowed the details about sleeping in a hollow log and being saved by noisy swine from the Flemings' account of their own escapes.
19. As with his wife, Williamson never names his father-in-law, making it impossible to track down any evidence of such a person in the relevant records.
20. Robert Hunter Morris served as governor of Pennsylvania from 1754 to 1756.
21. No such record of Williamson's interview with Morris exists.
22. At this time, the proprietor of Pennsylvania was Thomas Penn, son and heir to the colony's founder William Penn. Thomas Penn was the leader of the proprietary party in the colony's government, which sought to limit the taxation of proprietary lands and clashed with the Quaker party, which dominated the assembly and resisted declaring war on the Indians because of its commitment to pacifism. In this passage, Williamson is exhibiting familiarity with Pennsylvania's distinctive and factious politics, which he may have learned about while living in the colony or may have read about in the British press coverage of the Seven Years War.
23. As was the case with Williamson's alleged meeting with Governor Morris, there is no record of his appearance before the Pennsylvania assembly.
24. William Shirley was the royal governor of Massachusetts and commander of the 50th Regiment of Foot, a regular army unit based in New England that recruited American soldiers. After the death of Edward Braddock at the Battle of the Monongahela in July 1755, Shirley became commander-in-chief of British forces in North America until he was replaced by Lord Loudoun in 1756.

25. As was the case with his description of Philadelphia, Williamson plagiarized this description of Boston from the autobiographical narrative of Bampfylde-Moore Carew. See C. H. Wilkinson (ed.), *The King of the Beggars: Bampfylde-Moore Carew* (Oxford: Clarendon Press, 1931), 251–5.
26. Contemporary records offer no corroborating evidence for Williamson's story of the raid on the Long plantation and subsequent torture and rescue of their daughter. Its lurid detail and intimations of the young woman's sexual violation by her captors anticipates the sensationalism of captivity narratives from the Revolutionary and early national eras.
27. Oswego, established on the southeastern shore of Lake Ontario during the 1720s, served as a western fur trading post for New York and was strategically important because it was the only British outpost on the Great Lakes. William Shirley oversaw the construction of new fortifications there in 1755 and 1756, intending to use it as a base for launching attacks on the French at Fort Niagara to the west and Fort Frontenac to the north.
28. Catskill Mountains of eastern New York.
29. Williamson is referring to the Mohawk River, the water route used by the British to transport goods and soldiers west of Albany toward Oswego. Here he confuses the Mohawk, which flows east and is a tributary of the Hudson River, with the Allegheny River, which has its headwaters farther west in New York and flows into the Ohio River.
30. In describing the route from Albany to Oswego, Williamson confuses some place names but gets the general geography right. People and goods first moved overland from Albany to Schenectady, a Dutch town on the Mohawk River, then traveled upriver to the Great Carrying Place (modern Rome, New York), a portage from the Mohawk to Wood Creek. From Wood Creek, they resumed a water route, crossing Oneida Lake to the Oswego River, which Williamson calls the "*Alliganey*, or *Ohio* great river" here and the "*Onondago*" in the next paragraph. The Oswego River emptied into Lake Ontario, but travelers first had to portage around its falls approximately ten miles from the fort.
31. Colonel James Mercer was one of Shirley's subordinate officers. He was killed during the French siege of Oswego in August 1756.
32. Colonel Peter Schuyler was a militia officer who commanded New Jersey provincial troops stationed at Oswego in 1755 and 1756.
33. Now called the Oswego River.
34. The distance between Albany and Oswego is approximately 175 miles.
35. The St. Lawrence River.
36. Williamson dates the construction of these new forts a year too early. In 1755, Shirley ordered new fortifications built at Oswego: Fort Ontario on the east side of the Oswego River and Fort George (nicknamed Fort Rascal by the soldiers) on the west side, both intended to replace the decrepit original fort at the site.

37. There is no officer named King listed for the 50th Regiment in *By permission of the right honourable the Secretary at War. A List of the general and field-officers, as they rank in the Army* (London: J. Millan, [1756]).
38. Captain John Bradstreet of the 51st Regiment.
39. Dysentery.
40. The 51st Regiment, commanded by Sir William Pepperell.
41. Fort Niagara, the French post that guarded the passage between Lake Ontario and Lake Erie.
42. Fort Frontenac was the French post that guarded the passage from Lake Ontario to the St. Lawrence River, in present-day Kingston, Ontario.
43. Williamson is likely referring to William Johnson of New York, who like Shirley was charged with raising a provincial army in 1755 to move against the French along the New York–Canadian borderland. Johnson and Shirley competed against each other for Indian allies, and Shirley blamed the delays he encountered in launching an expedition against Fort Niagara in part on Johnson's machinations. Alternatively, Williamson may be referring in this passage to New York Governor James De Lancey, who also disliked Shirley and frustrated his efforts to provision the garrison at Oswego.
44. Fort Saint-Frédéric, also known as Crown Point, was a French post on Lake Champlain that guarded the passage from Albany to Montreal. It was the object of William Johnson's campaign in 1755.
45. Crown Point, also known as Fort St. Frédéric, was a French post on Lake Champlain. In 1755, William Johnson of New York raised an army of soldiers from the New England colonies to march against this post, but expedition stalled after the Battle of Lake George in September of that year.
46. In the Bay of Fundy campaign in 1755, British forces attacked French posts in Nova Scotia and initiated the expulsion of the French-speaking colonial population there known as the Acadians.
47. John Campbell, Earl of Loudoun replaced William Shirley as commander-in-chief of British forces in North America in 1756.
48. Louis Joseph, marquis de Montcalm replaced Jean-Armand Dieskau, Baron de Dieskau as the commander of French forces in North America after the latter was captured at the Battle of Lake George in September 1755.
49. John Shirley was William Shirley's son and an officer in the 50th Regiment. He died from a fatal case of dysentery he contracted at Oswego in 1755.
50. Major James Kinneer was an officer in the 50th Regiment.
51. The Moravians were a German-speaking pietist sect that settled in Pennsylvania's Lehigh Valley in the 1740s and started several mission communities among the Delaware Indians. One of these, Gnadenhütten, was attacked by hostile Indians in November 1755 and then again in January 1756.
52. The main Moravian settlement in the Lehigh Valley.
53. Williamson is here describing Indian raids on backcountry settlements in Pennsylvania during the fall of 1755 and winter of 1755–1756.

54. Scarouady (Oneida), also known as Monacatuatha, was a chief from Logstown, an Indian town in the Ohio country. Wary of the French at Fort Duquesne, he allied with the British during Braddock's campaign and tried to convince Pennsylvania to take up arms against the French and their Indian allies.
55. Conrad Weiser served Pennsylvania as an interpreter and diplomat to neighboring Indian nations. During the Seven Years War, he also served as a militia officer.
56. Pennsylvania, because of its Quaker origins, was the only colony in British North America without a militia. Benjamin Franklin drafted a bill to create such a voluntary force and the Pennsylvania Assembly passed it in late November 1755.
57. Williamson's description of his involvement in these events in Pennsylvania during the winter of 1755–1756 are plausible but not likely. If he had in fact been granted a leave from the 50th Regiment in New York to go home for the winter, he would have likely headed back to Chester County, Pennsylvania, where he had last lived as a civilian. It is more likely that he was among a detachment of soldiers from the 50th Regiment that was sent from New York City at this time by General Shirley to assist Pennsylvania governor Robert Hunter Morris with the defense of his colony. This group of soldiers spent three months in Reading and Easton, two towns then crowded with panicked refugees from the Indian raids on the frontier. It is highly unlikely that Williamson was recruited to join a Pennsylvania militia company because of his reputation as a skilled Indian fighter, as he describes here, although it should be noted that one such company did have a Lieutenant Patrick Davis as an officer.
58. Colonel John Armstrong was a Pennsylvania militia commander from Cumberland County. Williamson seems to be confusing his facts and timeline here. There was no Indian nation or group known as the "*Ohio Morians*," and Armstrong gained notoriety for leading an attack on the Delaware Indian town of Kittanning in September 1756.
59. "*Kennorton head*" appears to be a corruption of "Gnadenhütten," the Moravian community that Williamson referenced earlier.
60. As he had done with the story of the Long rescue earlier in his narrative, Williamson appears to have invented this story in order to illustrate for the reader his imagined prowess as an Indian fighter. No record exists of such an engagement at this time, in which a militia force lost forty-seven of its fifty men. Williamson likely based it on published reports of an Indian attack on a party of soldiers and laborers at Gnadenhütten on New Year's Day, 1756.
61. Benjamin Franklin led a militia force raised in Philadelphia in late 1755 and sent north to defend Berks and Northampton counties. Although eventually commissioned as a colonel, Franklin was derisively called "General Franklin" by the locals in this region.

62. Militia troops under Franklin's command did build Fort Allen, a defensive stockade, at the site of Gnadenhütten in January 1756.
63. Fort Norris was another stockade in Northampton County built by militia troops under Franklin's command.
64. A region in northeastern Northampton County near the Delaware River.
65. There is no evidence in contemporary records of the Indian attacks Williamson describes in this paragraph.
66. Fort Franklin was another stockade built during the winter of 1755–1756 by Pennsylvania militia troops, but it was located near a gap in the Blue Mountains west of Fort Allen, not in the Minisinks region.
67. There is no corroborating evidence in contemporary sources for the attack on the families of James Graham or Isaac Cook.
68. No such letter survives in the papers of Benjamin Franklin or other relevant sources. Williamson's account of his time as an Indian fighter attached to a Pennsylvania militia company would appear to be a self-aggrandizing fiction, but one given a sheen of verisimilitude because of his familiarity with place names and events in the region during the winter of 1755–1756.
69. The following three paragraphs describing the Kittanning Raid led by Pennsylvania militia officer John Armstrong in September 1756 are borrowed from the *Gentleman's Magazine* (London), February 1757 edition.
70. Fort Shirley was another Pennsylvania fort, built on a western tributary of the Susquehanna River.
71. James Hogg, a subordinate officer of Armstrong.
72. Captain Jacobs (Lenape), also known as Tewea, was a Delaware chief and leader of the Delaware town of Kittanning on the Allegheny River. He led raids against settlements in the Pennsylvanian backcountry after Braddock's Defeat, and his death was hailed as a great victory in the Pennsylvania press. Williamson later claimed to have received Captain Jacob's scalp as a gift from Benjamin Franklin and displayed it in his Edinburgh coffeehouse.
73. John Winslow commanded Massachusetts provincial troops during the Seven Years War.
74. In the spring of 1756, Colonel John Bradstreet did have command of the bateau men charged with transporting supplies from Albany to Oswego. There is no record of an engagement between these men and French-allied Indians at the Great Carrying Place on May 6 as Williamson describes, but Bradstreet was traveling with a convoy from Albany to Oswego at that time, and Williamson may very well have been wounded in the manner he describes here. After he returned to Aberdeen, two officers he had served under testified that he had been wounded during his service.
75. Williamson's story about the soldier who survived his own scalping is corroborated in journals kept by Stephen Cross, a civilian contractor at Oswego, and Patrick Mackellar, an army engineer, both of which date the incident to the night of May 24, 1756.

76. General James Abercromby was Lord Loudoun's second-in-command of British forces in North America in 1756.
77. Sir Peter Halkett commanded the 44th Regiment but was killed at the Battle of the Monongahela in 1755. Colonel Thomas Dunbar commanded the 48th Regiment. Both regiments had come to America as part of the Braddock campaign against Fort Duquesne, a year before the siege of Oswego.
78. Pierre de Rigaud de Vaudreuil de Cavagnial, marquis de Vaudreuil was governor-general of New France from 1755 until 1760.
79. This is a swipe at William Shirley, who had served on an Anglo-French commission in Paris after the War of the Austrian Succession (1740–1748) to settle borders between French and British possessions in North America.
80. The French forces at the siege of Oswego totaled approximately 3000 regulars, Canadian *troupes de la marine*, and militiamen, as well as 300 Indian warriors.
81. Modern Chaumont Bay on Lake Ontario.
82. Williamson's description of the siege and fall of Oswego as conveyed in the following paragraphs is borrowed mostly from a summary published in the *Gentleman's Magazine* (London) in its November 1756 and February 1757 editions.
83. Captain Housman Broadley commanded the small fleet of British vessels at Oswego.
84. Colonel Patrick Mackellar, a British military engineer at Oswego.
85. Lieutenant Colonel John Littlehales took over command after Mercer's death and negotiated the garrison's surrender to Montcalm.
86. General Daniel Webb, a subordinate officer of Lord Loudoun.
87. A colonial settlement in the western Mohawk Valley.
88. The French post guarding the passage from Lake Champlain to Lake George.
89. Williamson is referring here to the British loss of Fort William Henry on Lake George in 1757.
90. Williamson's description of his return to Britain and discharge from the army is corroborated by other evidence. The *La Renommé* was the first ship to sail from Quebec with prisoners of war from Oswego. According to a return prepared by Colonel Littlehales, it carried 332 officers and enlisted men from the 50th and 51st regiments. After a five-week voyage, the ship arrived at Plymouth on November 6, 1756. A month later, the Crown decided to break the 50th and 51st regiments and draft their able-bodied men into other regiments then being deployed to America. Williamson was apparently among the wounded and disabled men who were discharged in March 1757.
91. "A Discourse on Kidnapping" first appeared in the third edition of *French and Indian Cruelty*, published in Glasgow in 1758. The version here is considerably expanded from the original by Williamson's inclusion of excerpts

from the depositions of witnesses who testified in his lawsuit against the Aberdeen magistrates.
92. Fined.
93. The letter of recantation that Williamson claims he was forced to sign by the magistrates was published in the *Aberdeen Journal* on June 27, 1758.
94. A solicitor in Edinburgh's courts.
95. Before departing for the colonies, indentured servants were expected to appear before a local magistrate or justice of the peace to swear that they had entered into their contracts willingly.
96. This summary of Williamson's lawsuit against the Aberdeen magistrates first appeared in the fifth edition of *French and Indian Cruelty*.
97. Edinburgh attorney Andrew Crosbie.
98. This was the account book (what Williamson called the "kidnapping book") that detailed the recruitment of servants for the *Planter*.
99. Walter Scott (1729–1799) was the father of the novelist Sir Walter Scott and a member of the Writers to the Signet, a professional organization of solicitors in Edinburgh.

Index

50th Regiment, xiii, 23, 53
51st Regiment, 33

Aberdeen, vii, xv, 4; *see also* indentured servants, trade in
Aberdeen Journal, 74
Aboyne, 4
Abernethy, James, 83, 92
Adams, John, 12
Alamingo, 15, 18
Albany, 35
American coffeehouse, viii
Annesley, James, xiv
Armstrong, Colonel John, 42, 45–6

Bell, John, 21–2
Berks County, 7
Bethlehem, 39
Black, George, 92
Blue Hills, 10, 11, 19, 42, 43
Boone, Daniel, xviii
Boston, 24–5
Braddock, General Edward, xii, 36–7, 40
Bradley, Captain Housman, 51, 57
Brand, Robert, 88–9
Broadstreet, Captain John, 32, 47, 49–50
Burnet, John, 81, 82, 83, 86–8

Campbell, Colonel James, 56
Canada, 69–70

Cannocojigge, 13, 19
Cape May, xii, 4–5, 96
Carolina, 68–9
Chester County, xiii, 22
Cochran, Walter, x, 94–5, 100
Cook, Isaac, 45
Cooper, James Fenimore, xiv
Court of Session, ix, xi, 74, 99
Crawford, James, 25–8
Crosbie, Andrew, ix
Crown Point, 37

Davidson, William, 99–100
Davis, Captain, 42
Defoe, Daniel, xiv
Dickson, John, 96
Dieskau, Major General Jean-Armand, Baron de, 37

Edinburgh, viii, 98
Elphingston, John, 80, 81, 83, 92, 94
Elmsie brothers, 81, 82

factual fictions, xiv–xv
Finlater, Christian, 88
Folke, George, 13
Fort Allen, 44
Fort Duquesne, 18
Fort Franklin, 44
Fort Frontenac, 35, 37, 47
Fort George, 58; *see also* Fort William Henry

Fort Norris, 43, 44
Fort Ontario, 52–3
Fort Shirley, 45–6
Fort William Henry, xiii; see also Fort George
Franklin, Benjamin, xiii, 43–5
Fraser, Francis, 81
French and Indian Cruelty, vii–ix, xii
   as literature, xiv–xix
   frontispiece, xv–xvii
   publication history, xvii–xviii

Garioch, George, 90–1, 92
Gibson, William, 96
Gnadenhutten, 39, 42–3; see also Kennorton head
Gordon, Alexander, 91–2
Graham, James, 44
Gray, Alexander, 84–5, 92
Great Carrying Place, 29, 33, 47, 58
Great Cove, 39
Great Swamp, 12
Grigerson, Alexander, 84

Hamilton, Captain Archibald, 56
Hirnley, 4
Hogg, Lieutenant James, 45

indentured servants
   life in America, 77–9
   trade in, 71–96
Indians see Native Americans
Ingram, James, 84–5
Iroquois confederacy, 30

Jacobs, Captain, 46
Jamieson, William and John, 86–8
Johnston, George, 82–3
Jopp, James, 99–100

Kennorton head, 42–3; see also Gnaddenhutten
kidnapping, viii, 4, 71–96
kidnapping book, x, 95
Kimber, Edward, xiv
King, Alexander, 79–80
Kinneer, Major James, 37, 45
Kittanning, 45–6

La Renomme, 70
Law, Helen, 83, 92–3, 94
Lehigh Valley, xii
Leslie, George, 88
Lewis, John, 13
Ley, Peter, 81, 82
Littlehales, Lieutenant Colonel John, 55
Long, Joseph, 25
   daughter's captivity and rescue, 25–8
Loudoun, John Campbell, Earl of, 37, 50, 58

MacKellar, Colonel Patrick, 53
Mackie, George, 89–90
Mackie, Hugh, 88
Maryland, 67–8
Mercer, Colonel James, 29, 51–4
Miller, Jacob, 13
Minisinkes, 64
Monongahela, Battle of the, xii, 36
Monokatoathy see Scarrooyda
Montcalm, General Louis Joseph, marquis de, xiii, 37, 51–6
Montreal, 57
Moraley, William, xiv–xv
Moravians, 39, 42
Morris, Robert Hunter, 22

Native Americans
   alliance and trade with, 59–64
   culture of, 15–18
   education, manners, and religion of, 30–1
   methods of warfare, 60–1
New England, 64–5
New York (colony), 65
New York City, 37–8
Niagara, 34, 35, 37
Nova Scotia, 37, 69

Oswego, xiii
   campaign of 1755, 28–9, 32–5
   campaign of 1756, 47–50
   consequences of fall of, 58–9
   fortifications at, 48
   massacre at, 55–6
   siege of, 51–7
   terms of capitulation, 55

Pennsylvania, 66–7
Pennsylvania Assembly, 38, 40–1
  Williamson's interview with, 23
Pepperrell, Sir William, 33
Philadelphia, 5–6, 40
Planter, The, x, xi, xiii, 96
Plymouth, vii, xv, 70

Quebec, xiv, 57

Ragg, Captain Robert, x, 92–3, 94, 95, 96
Rattary, James, 90
Reid, Margaret, 82
Reid, Robert, 81
Robertson, James, 93–4
Ross, Margaret, 84–6

scalping
  bounties for, 67
  described, 11n
  Irish soldier survives, 48–9
Scarrooyda, 40–1
Schuyler, Colonel Peter, 29, 53–4
Scott, Sir Walter (1771–1832), xx
Scott, Walter (1729–1799), 99
Seven Years War, vii
Sheds, James and William, 82
Shirley, Captain John, 37
Shirley, General William, xiii, 23, 50
Smith, James, x, 81, 92, 94–5
Smollett, Tobias, xx
Snider, Jacob, 10
Stevenson, Robert Louis, xx
Susquehanna River, 10, 12, 13
Swift, Jonathan, xiv

Ticonderoga, 58
tomahawk, description of, 9n
Transportation Act, xi
Travels of Peter Williamson, ix
Tulpehockin, 39

Vaudreuil, Pierre de Rigaud, 51
Virginia, 68, 82–3
Vitree, Captain Dennis, 70

Webb, General Daniel, 58
Weiser, Conrad, 40, 66
wigwams, description of, 15n
Williamson, James, 79–80, 81, 82
Williamson, Peter, vii–xx
  author, printer, and bookseller, xviii–xix
  birth and family, 3–4
  death and burial, xix
  divorce, xix
  in America, xii–xiv
  Indian captivity of, xii, 8–23
  kidnapping, ix–xii, 4
  lawsuit against Aberdeen magistrates, 97–102
  marriage in America, 7–8, 22
  military service of, xiii–xiv, 23–57, 70
  prisoner of war, 57–8, 70
  prosecuted for libel, 71–4
  voyage to America, 4–5
Wilson, Hugh, xii–xiii, 5–6
Wilson, Isabel, 81–2
Wilson, James, 88
Wilson, John, 80
Winslow, General John, 47, 58

York, 70

EU representative:
Easy Access System Europe
Mustamäe tee 50, 10621 Tallinn, Estonia
Gpsr.requests@easproject.com